THE POWER OF
FORGIVENESS

THE POWER OF
FORGIVENESS

HOW TO GET ALONG
WITH EVERYBODY
ALL THE TIME!

HAROLD VAUGHAN

DESTINY IMAGE® PUBLISHERS, INC.
P.O. Box 310, Shippensburg, PA 17257-0310
"Promoting Inspired Lives."

This book and all other Destiny Image and Destiny Image Fiction books are available at Christian bookstores and distributors worldwide.

For more information on foreign distributors, call 717-532-3040.
Reach us on the Internet: www.destinyimage.com.

ISBN 13 TP: 978-0-7684-6294-4
ISBN 13 eBook: 978-0-7684-6295-1

For Worldwide Distribution, Printed in the U.S.A.
1 2 3 4 5 6 7 8 / 26 25 24 23 22

CONTENTS

Preface 1

SECTION 1 Granting Forgiveness. 3

CHAPTER 1 Why Should I Forgive?. 5

CHAPTER 2 What Is Forgiveness? 13

CHAPTER 3 What If I Don't Want to Forgive? 27

CHAPTER 4 How Does Unforgiveness Give Ground
to Satan? 37

CHAPTER 5 You've Convinced Me—but
Where Do I Start? 47

CHAPTER 6 Why Is It So Hard to Forgive? 55

CHAPTER 7 What Should I Do When I'm
Tempted to Unforgive? 65

SUMMARY OF SECTION 1 Practical Steps to Forgiving Others . . .73

SECTION 2 Seeking Forgiveness. 77

CHAPTER 8 Is It Really Necessary to Ask
for Forgiveness?. .79

CHAPTER 9 But What If...?. 85

CHAPTER 10 How Can I Tell If My Conscience
Is Violated? 93

CHAPTER 11 How Do I Clear My Conscience?. 103

CHAPTER 12   How Do I Ask for Forgiveness? 111

SUMMARY OF SECTION 2   Practical Steps When Seeking
                           Forgiveness 117

SECTION 3   Scrutinizing Forgiveness 121

CHAPTER 13   Are Forgiveness and Reconciliation
                 the Same Thing? .123

CHAPTER 14   What About Brawlers? 131

CHAPTER 15   How to Get Beyond Your Hurts. 137

CHAPTER 16   Cut or Untangle? 145

CHAPTER 17   What Is Jesus' Strategy for Restoration? . . . 151

SUMMARY OF SECTION 3   Summarizing the Difference between
                           Forgiveness and Reconciliation. 159

SECTION 4   Enjoying Forgiveness. 161

CHAPTER 18   What Are the Fruits of Forgiveness? 163

CHAPTER 19   Has God Forgiven You? 173

CHAPTER 20   How Do I Know I Have Forgiven? 179

SUMMARY OF SECTION 4   Closing Summary 189

                           References. 191

PREFACE

So many have been hurt, abused, betrayed, and devastated by the actions of others. These wounds have left tremendous injuries and damaging divisions. The Bible prescribes the cure in such cases: forgiveness and reconciliation. As our culture continues to disintegrate, I can think of no greater truth that needs to be practiced than forgiveness.

In his book *Mere Christianity*, C. S. Lewis wrote, "Forgiveness is a beautiful word until you have something to forgive." Lofty concepts like forgiveness are appealing in a theoretical sense but can be difficult when applied practically and personally.

God has not promised utopia in this life. Offenses will come. When offenses come, we must know and *practice* the art of forgiveness. Other times we are the offenders, and we must seek reconciliation. This book is an instruction manual on forgiveness. It also addresses how to relate to our offenders who remain unrepentant.

Through Calvary, forgiveness has become a blessed reality. Healing, liberation, and lasting freedom can be ours by practicing this skill. It is my desire that many will be set free by the truths presented in this book.

If the title seems a bit too promising, hold off judgment until you have read the book. Through grace, obedience, and wisdom, we can do our part in getting along with others, even if they refuse to get along with us!

HAROLD VAUGHAN

GRANTING FORGIVENESS

CHAPTER 1

WHY SHOULD I FORGIVE?

I heard of a man who was bitten by a rabid dog. The attending doctor told him that rabies was not only incurable, it was also fatal. The physician recommended that the dying man get his house in order. Both shocked and silent, the patient just sat there. At length, the doomed man requested a pen and paper. He started then to write fast and furiously. About an hour later, the doctor came by and found the man still writing feverishly. The doctor said, "I'm glad to see you are writing out your will." The man responded, "This ain't no will. It's a list of all the people I'm going to bite before I die!" Living with bitterness is a poor way to exist, and dying with bitterness is the worst way to exit the planet. So why should we forgive our offenders?

The way we treat our fellow men is a clear indicator of our relationship with God. The Lord Jesus takes the way we treat others personally: *"Inasmuch as ye have done it unto one of the least of these my brethren, ye have done it unto me"* (Matt. 25:40). Consequently, to be at odds with a fellow Christian spells double trouble: not only are we at odds with our brother, but we are also at odds with Christ in him. The converse is true as well: *"Inasmuch as ye did it not to one of the least of these, ye did it not to me"* (Matt. 25:45). The Lord documents our dealings with others. The way we relate to the *"least of these"* is of utmost importance to God. Our treatment of others indicates what we think about Christ.

So important is forgiveness that Jesus emphasized it in the model prayer: *"And forgive us our debts, as we forgive our debtors"* (Matt. 6:12). Jesus' words could not be plainer: *"For if ye forgive men their trespasses, your heavenly Father will also forgive you: But if ye forgive not men their trespasses, neither will your Father forgive your trespasses"* (Matt. 6:14-15). There is a correlation between our treatment of others and God's treatment of us.

The model prayer gives us instruction on how we should speak with God. And before we can speak with the Lord, we must deal with the vital subject of forgiveness: *"And forgive us our debts, as we forgive our debtors"* (Matt. 6:12). This first part of the model prayer addresses vertical forgiveness: *"Forgive us our debts"* (Matt. 6:12).

Keeping short accounts with God by admitting and confessing our sins is imperative:

> *If we say that we have fellowship with him, and walk in darkness, we lie, and do not the truth: But if we walk in the light, as he is in the light, we have fellowship one with another, and the blood of Jesus Christ his Son cleanseth us from all sin. If we say that we have no sin, we deceive ourselves, and the truth is not in us. If we confess our sins, he is faithful and just to forgive us our sins, and to cleanse us from all unrighteousness* (1 John 1:6-9).

Walking in the light means putting every *dark thing* under Christ's blood. Fellowship with God is possible because divine mercy has paid the price for our forgiveness, that is, Christ's death on the cross. While a Christian has perfect *standing* before God, his *state* is dependent on his willingness to visit the fountain filled with blood as often as sin arises. We must put our sins where God put them, beneath Christ's atoning blood. Calvary covers our sins from God's viewpoint. But we must uncover our transgressions through confession to maintain fellowship with God. Since Christ emphasized this essential category of divine forgiveness in the model prayer, it must be vitally important and foundational. Agreeing with God about our sin is the meaning of confession. And when we confess our wrongs to God, He faithfully restores our fellowship and vital reality.

On the heels of vertical forgiveness is horizontal forgiveness: *"...as we forgive our debtors"* (Matt. 6:12). Forgiven people are forgiving people! As we receive God's forgiveness for our offenses, we are enabled to forgive our offenders. One mark of saving grace is the imparted capacity to extend forgiveness to others. As grace comes into us, grace flows out from us. When mercy is experienced, mercy is extended. The cross points in two directions: vertically and horizontally. Meaningful prayer is contingent upon forgiveness.

Next to loving God with all our heart, mind, and strength, our foremost priority is relating properly to our fellow man. Jesus spelled it out clearly: *"Therefore if thou bring thy gift to the altar, and there rememberest that thy brother hath ought against thee; leave there thy gift before the altar, and go thy way; **first be reconciled** to thy brother, and then come and offer thy gift"* (Matt. 5:23-24, emphasis added). Reconciliation is God's priority for you and me. It precedes giving, service, and sacrifice. It is so important that Jesus said we should *"leave there*

[our] *gift"* and *"first be reconciled."* Before giving and serving, our Lord demands reconciliation. But why?

The Old Testament declares that any high priest who touched a dead animal was ceremonially unclean. Once defiled, he was not allowed to carry out his priestly duties until he had gone through a purification process. Touching a dead animal would not in itself prevent the priest from carrying out his duties. Efficiency was not the issue. He could have easily gone through the motions, but his service was unacceptable to God because he was personally contaminated. Here is a worthy principle: the acceptability of any gift or service is determined by the acceptability of the giver. If the giver is unfit, the gift is unacceptable, even abominable in God's sight. God will not accept a gift if the giver is personally contaminated by broken relationships.

This is the reason why God has said we must first *attempt* to be reconciled. Let me emphasize the word *attempt*. Broken relationships so contaminate us before God that our service is unacceptable. Therefore, we must first seek reconciliation. As Christians, our vertical relationship with God is affected by our horizontal relationships with others. If we are to stabilize our relationship with God, often we must begin by first stabilizing horizontal relationships. Yes, we must do all in our power to put things right, even though we have no control over how others will respond or react. The difference between reconciliation and forgiveness will be closely examined in later chapters.

The word *reconciliation* means "to be at peace with." Our fallen nature is at enmity with God, but the Lord Jesus has reconciled people to God by His death on the cross. The enmity is gone once we are saved; we are at peace with God. Reconciliation means putting things right when things have gone wrong. When it comes to our attention that we have offended someone, intentionally or unintentionally, knowingly or unknowingly, willingly or unwillingly, it is our responsibility to drop everything and go to the offended party. Then, in humility and sincerity, we are to seek to restore the relationship. The response of the offended party may be positive or negative. But once we obey God, we are free, and the offended party's response is between him and God. Our sole duty is obedience.

Scripture teaches the importance of forgiveness and reconciliation. To be *on the outs* on earth means we are out of touch with heaven. God admonishes us to keep lines of open communication in marriage *"that* [our] *prayers be not hindered"* (1 Pet. 3:7). For example, when married couples are not on speaking terms with each other, they may not be on speaking terms with God.

Herein lies the root of much spiritual sickness. Few realize how unforgiveness, hurt feelings, and adverse relationships dramatically affect our relationship with God. The Apostle John said, "*...for he that loveth not his brother whom he hath seen, how can he love God whom he hath not seen?*" (1 John 4:20). In other words, if we cannot properly relate to human beings, how can we pretend to be rightly relating to God?

Jesus said, "*...first be reconciled*" (Matt. 5:24) because reconciliation and forgiveness are first on Jesus' list. They must be first on ours as well. We will see clearly the importance of forgiveness in subsequent chapters, which discuss in more detail the consequences of not forgiving.

REFLECTIONS

1. The way we treat our fellow man is a direct gauge of our relationship with God. The Lord Jesus takes the way we treat others personally.

2. Forgiveness is so vital to a believer's walk that Jesus included it in the model prayer: "*And forgive us our debts, as we forgive our debtors*" (Matt. 6:12). Forgiven people have the capacity to forgive those who offend them.

3. The acceptability of any gift is determined by the acceptability of the giver.

4. When the fact that we have offended someone, intentionally or unintentionally, knowingly or unknowingly, willingly or unwillingly, comes to our attention, our responsibility is to drop everything and go to the offended party. Obedience is proof of our devotion to Christ.

STUDY QUESTIONS AND POINTS OF APPLICATION

1. The first directives in Scripture focus on God's priorities for our lives. Describe why forgiving our offenders is on God's priority list for us.

2. Identify any relationships in your life where forgiveness is needed.

3. Attempting reconciliation with others, when a relational breakdown occurs, is the outgrowth of redemption. What is the essential meaning of the word *reconciliation?*

4. Do you need to seek reconciliation with anyone?

CHAPTER 2

WHAT IS FORGIVENESS?

A little girl was attempting to pray a portion of the model prayer. She said, "And forgive us of our trash baskets as we forgive those who put trash in our baskets." She got a bit mixed up over the word *trespasses* but her version has some validity. When people put "trash in our baskets," we have to deal with it. This is the heart of forgiveness: dealing with the trash that comes our way.

Misconceptions about forgiveness abound. Someone described it this way: "Forgiveness is healing others by using their offenses as the means to express Christ's love." The nature of forgiveness is so radical that forgiveness is an abstract ideal in the minds of many. Often, we can come closer to understanding what something is by defining what it is *not*. The following truths address misunderstandings about forgiveness.

Forgiveness is not an emotion. Some believe that forgiveness is primarily an emotion. But our feelings, in fact, are irrelevant. While suspended on Calvary's cross, Jesus prayed, *"Father, forgive them…"* (Luke 23:34). Physically tortured, spiritually tormented, and mentally tried, the Lord Jesus chose to forgive. His request was obviously an act of His will, not just an emotional outburst. Stephen, while being stoned to death, prayed and asked God to forgive his bloodthirsty accusers, to *"lay not this sin to their charge"* (Acts 7:60). In its initial stage, forgiveness is definitely not an emotion; we can grant it despite our feelings. So don't wait for a warm fuzzy to overwhelm you before you forgive. If you wait for some emotion, you may wait forever!

Forgiveness is not forgetting. How often have we heard, "If you didn't forget it, you really didn't forgive it"? That's the most absurd counsel anyone can give. Forgiveness is not erasing unpleasant and painful memories. It is humanly impossible to blot out unwanted memories at will. Almighty God is the only One who has the ability to willingly forget. Only He could say, *"I will forgive their iniquity, and I will remember their sin no more"* (Jer. 31:34).

On a human level, forgetting has nothing to do with forgiving. We've all had things happen to us that we will never forget while we live on this planet. Thankfully, that fact has nothing to do with forgiveness. Time does not heal all hurts. But forgiveness is the doorway that puts us well on our way to the healing process. Once forgiveness is granted, recurring thoughts about the episode may, and probably will, return. This does not mean that we were insincere. Although we may not be able to forget completely, the frequency with which those thoughts come to mind will decrease once we decide to forgive. As we practice the freedom of forgiveness, the intervals between remembrances will lengthen. And when an incident does come to mind, we will know how to handle it.

Forgiveness is not pretending that nothing happened or attempting to bury the pain. It is not just letting the offense slide or taking a neutral position. Being neutral is not a possibility. God expects us to respond properly. As we shall see, forgiveness is far more than doing nothing. It also doesn't mean that we passively tolerate future abuse or dismiss the offender's moral responsibility. Forgiveness is not an agreement to trust an untrustworthy person.

Forgiveness is not asking God to forgive the person who hurt you. That idea, though commendable, is not forgiveness. In fact, you can only pray, *"Father, forgive them; for they know not what they do...*" (Luke 23:34) with meaning after you have forgiven the offender yourself. When Jesus prayed, He had no malice in His heart. The crucifixion was the *"cup"* (Matt. 26:39) He had to drink. When He prayed on the cross, He was not trying to empty His soul of anger; His was an honest prayer of concern for the salvation of His abusers.

Forgiveness is not asking God to forgive you for being hurt, angry, and upset. While we need to take responsibility for our attitudes and actions, this step is secondary. If someone offended you, forgiving that particular person is a must. You must deal with God about your resentment. But you must also deal with the offense and the person who hurt you.

Forgiveness is not rationalizing or understanding why the person acted toward you as he did. What he did and why he did it are irrelevant. Understanding the reasons why your offender did what he did is unnecessary and isn't forgiveness.

SO, WHAT IS FORGIVENESS?

First, forgiveness is a choice. It is nothing less than a decisive act of the will. In Matthew 18, Jesus spoke of a certain king who took account of his servants and found one who owed him a mountain of money. Apparently, he had squandered his master's investments. The king commanded that the slave, his family, and his belongings be sold to pay the debt. The servant pleaded for more time and told the king he would pay him back, but he could never have paid it all back. He was so far in debt that repayment was out of the question. Nevertheless, his pleading paid off. The king forgave the debt and set him free.

This forgiven, liberated servant promptly went out and arrested a fellow slave. He took this fellow slave by the throat and demanded payment of the few dollars owed to him. The indebted servant fell on his knees and begged for time to pay the debt. This plea was within the realm of possibility; in time, he could have paid what he owed. But the first servant wouldn't listen, and he had the second man thrown into the debtors' prison. Here is a man who, released from a staggering debt, refused to forgive his fellow slave for an insignificant sum.

The king called in the first servant. After telling him that he was a wicked servant, the king harshly rebuked him and delivered him to the tormentors until such time as he had paid all that was due. Jesus concluded by warning that our Heavenly Father will do the same to us if we refuse to forgive those who wrong us.

This story teaches us that forgiveness is a decision to release others from the debts they owe us. When we refuse to forgive, we put the unforgiven party in debtors' prison. Let me illustrate. Suppose I was your pastor, and somehow I offended you. Perhaps I made a decision you didn't agree with, or I didn't recognize some sacrifice you had made for the church. Perhaps I failed to visit you when you were sick. When you see me, that offense is all you think about. You have bound me and put me in debtors' prison. I may even ask for forgiveness, but unless you release me from that debt, I can bless and help others, but I cannot help you. In your eyes, everything I do is tainted by that one act of injury. By refusing to forgive me, you bind me from being what God wants me to be in your life. When you fail to forgive and refuse to release a debt, you put others into debtors' prison. Though not a physical prison, it is real nonetheless. Holding those offenses against me lands me in the position of a debtor, and one from which I cannot escape without your consent. You have bound me in debtors' prison.

When I started to consider the subject of forgiveness seriously, I made a shocking discovery. What came to my attention was that most of us have an *accounts-receivable book*. I am not referring to a balance sheet on a businessman's computer. This accounts-receivable sheet is filed away in the human heart. Every time others offend us, down the offense goes. It is recorded. They owe us. We are holding a debt against them. I'm not talking about an *I-owe-you*. It's a *You-owe-me* list. When your mate crosses you, down it goes: "I'll remember that," you say to yourself. If the pastor offends us, we promptly enter his offense on the balance sheet. When our children embarrass us, down it goes. "I'll remember that next time they want to go out for ice cream." When people wrong us, we place them on the accounts-receivable list. They are in debt to us; they owe us.

Many would be willing to forgive, if their transgressors would apologize. But I have good news! You do not need to wait for an apology to forgive someone. Wicked scoffers mocked Jesus when He hung on the cross. None of them offered an apology. Yet Jesus ask the Father to forgive them (Luke 23:34). How others respond or fail to respond makes no difference; you can release others from their debts whenever you choose. You need not wait for an apology.

Forgiveness is a decision to shred the You-owe-me list. It is a deliberate choice to release people from the debt they owe you. Bitterness will dry up the river of blessing and zap your joy. Norman Cousins commented, "Life is an adventure in forgiveness." Shredding that list turns a miserable journey into a joy ride.

Do you have a you-owe-me list? Here's how to shred it. Go to the Lord in prayer and tell Him you are making choices to forgive. Here's an example:

Lord, I am making a decision to forgive my friend for breaking a confidence. Lord, the offense hurt me but I will never hold it against him again. I release him from that debt. I forgive him.

Continue to pray and don't stop until you have shredded your entire list. You should confess and forsake every resentment against your parents, children, family members, friends, neighbors, church members, employers, employees, and enemies.

In his book, *Mistreated*, Ron Lee Davis wrote the following:

> Some years ago, a millionaire—let's call him Mr. Yale—owned a lot in an exclusive residential area of a large city. This lot presented an unusual problem because it was only a couple yards wide by nearly a hundred feet long. Clearly, there was nothing he could do with such an oddly proportioned piece of real estate but sell it to one of the neighbors on either side. So Mr. Yale went first to Mr. Smith, the neighbor on the east side of the lot, and asked if he would be interested in buying it.
>
> "Well," said Mr. Smith, "I really wouldn't have much use for it. But I'll tell you what,

since you're in something of a bind, I'd be willing to take it off your hands—purely as a favor, of course." Then he named a ridiculously low price.

"A favor, you say!" Yale exploded. "Why, that's not even one-tenth what the lot is worth!"

"That's all it's worth to me, and that's my offer."

Yale stormed out and went to see the neighbor on the west side, Mr. Jones. To Yale's dismay, Jones bettered the previous offer by only a few dollars. "Look, Yale," Jones said smugly, "I've got you over a barrel and you know it. You can't sell that lot to anyone else and you can't build on it. So there's my offer. Take it or leave it."

"So you think I'm over a barrel?" Yale retorted. "I'll show you no one can cheat me!"

"What are you going to do?"

Yale grinned maliciously. "You just wait!"

Within a few days, the embittered millionaire hired an architect and a contractor to build one of the strangest houses ever conceived. Only five feet wide and running the full length of his property, Yale's house was little more than a row of claustrophobic rooms, each barely able to accommodate a stick of furniture. As the house went up, the neighbors complained that the bizarre structure would blight the neighborhood, but city officials could find no code or regulation to disallow it.

When it was finished, Yale moved into his uncomfortable and impractical house, a self-condemned man in a prison of revenge. There he stayed for many years. Finally, he died there. The house, which became known in the neighborhood as "Spite House," still stands as a monument to one man's hate.

Unforgiveness is a two-way street. If you decide to put someone in debtors' prison, God will do the same to you. Jesus said His Heavenly Father will bind and deliver you to the tormentors. (See Matthew 18:34.) When unforgiveness occurs, the Lord places you in debtors' prison: in a spiritual vacuum. He will not release you until you choose to forgive others. Unconfessed animosity shuts down your spiritual life. You cannot pray, witness, or worship. Your spiritual life will shrivel and die. This condition demonstrates the *reap-what-you-sow* principle. God responds to you in the same way you respond to others. Unforgiveness not only imprisons those indebted to us but also sentences us to the same place where we have placed others. Forgiveness is the obligation of the forgiven. When we forgive, we set a prisoner free. Then we discover *we* were that prisoner.

Reconciliation must be initiated by the person to whom God speaks. It is not a matter of meeting someone halfway or waiting for him to approach you. Once God calls a conflict to your attention, leave your gift, go your way, and seek reconciliation. Two ladies in a church were at odds and everyone knew it. The Lord spoke to one of them. She went to the other lady and, by humbling herself, was able to resolve the conflict. When God speaks, you must respond. You don't need to search for these incidents; God will point them out. Then, after God speaks, you must be the one who initiates reconciliation.

Years ago, I took some clothes to a local dry cleaner. Not only did I take clothes to the cleaners, but I was also *taken to the cleaners* on the same trip. After returning home with the clothes, I discovered that the pants were torn and a necktie was shredded. *No problem*, I thought. *I'll just take them back and get reimbursed.* So I gathered my damaged clothes and went back to the dry cleaner. I showed the clerk my ruined garments and expected repayment. The clerk, however, informed me that the manager who took care of those incidents was unavailable. "No problem," I said. "When will he be in?" She gave me a time. I went back but he still wasn't in. I am a little slow in catching on. After five return visits, I began to see an emerging pattern. That local business intended to beat me out of any reimbursement. I was furious! My first thought was to take out a newspaper advertisement and warn the public about the business establishment. Then I discovered that the advertisement would have been illegal. Next, I thought about printing a handbill and warning all potential customers by stationing myself on the sidewalk immediately outside the dry cleaner. But I didn't have time for that.

By now, you can see that I was angry, very angry. I had been cheated. I was getting nowhere on a human level, so I decided to utilize a spiritual approach. This verse came to mind, *"Vengeance is mine; I will repay, saith the Lord"* (Rom. 12:19).

I prayed, "Lord, let them have it! Strike them down!" Every time I drove by, I glanced over to see whether the place had been struck by lightning the night before! I was really mad. I had sought justice, but I did not find it.

That is often the case in this fallen world. There is nothing wrong with seeking justice, but often it is elusive. I was left with two choices: get bitter or forgive. Being bitter is a sin, so I chose (though I didn't feel like it) to forgive. I released the debt and turned the offending party over to God. I was never reimbursed and I never received an apology. That doesn't matter now. The decision to forgive released me from my prison of bitterness. As someone once said, "The biblical attitude for forgiveness: grant it when it is requested; give it when it is not."

REFLECTIONS

1. Forgiveness is not an emotion. Neither is it forgetting, pretending that nothing happened, asking God to forgive you for being hurt, or understanding your offender's motives.

2. Forgiveness is a choice to release a debt. Failure to forgive puts your offender in debtors' prison.

3. God treats us the way we treat others. When we place others in debtors' prison, the Lord places us in debtors' prison. We are bound up until we release others.

4. "The biblical attitude for forgiveness: grant it when it is requested; give it when it is not."

STUDY QUESTIONS AND POINTS OF APPLICATION

1. When our minds accept wrong concepts, to that degree we are deceived. From the list of misconceptions about forgiveness, which ones have been part of your thinking?

2. Purpose to reject wrong thinking about forgiveness and ask God to give you discernment. Take time to relate these faulty views to specific people and events in your life.

3. Wrong thinking, when believed and acted upon, brings destructive consequences. What harsh chastening does God bring when we fail to forgive others?

4. Compile your You-owe-me list and *shred it!*

CHAPTER 3

WHAT IF I DON'T WANT TO FORGIVE?

While it is true that forgiveness is costly, unforgiveness is even more costly. In the final analysis, both are costly but in entirely different ways. Though forgiveness is painful in the initial stages, the ultimate end is healing. When someone hurts us, forgiveness means giving up our right to hurt that person back. On the other hand, unforgiveness produces immediate bitterness and spiritual barrenness now, and, ultimately, it leads to a host of other destructive consequences. As Nelson Mandela once said, "Bitterness is a poison you drink that kills you before the other man dies." What are the results of that corrosive culprit called *bitterness*?

The first consequence of not forgiving is spiritual death. As we have already seen, when we don't forgive others, God withholds grace from us. We cannot overstate the seriousness of this truth. Unforgiveness is unforgivable! A person who *cannot* forgive is a person who has not been forgiven. When God, in mercy, saves a lost soul, He implants within that soul the ability to forgive. I am not saying that a Christian is incapable of harboring resentment. But *cannot forgive* and *will not forgive* are two different things. A true Christian *can* forgive when he chooses. Unforgiveness in a child of God is an awful thing. It kills every ounce of spiritual vitality. How often have you witnessed the deterioration and plummet of a bitter Christian? He who does not forgive destroys the bridge over which he, himself, must pass. As long as he covers his sin, he cannot prosper. (See Proverbs 28:13.)

Mark makes a definite connection between unforgiveness and unanswered prayer: "*What things soever ye desire, when ye pray, believe that ye receive them, and ye shall have them. And when ye stand praying, forgive, if ye have ought against any: that your Father also which is in heaven may forgive you your trespasses*" (Mark 11:24-25). This great prayer promise concludes with a condition and a serious warning: "...*forgive...that your Father also which is in heaven may forgive you your trespasses*" (Mark 11:25). Unforgiveness bars God from even hearing our prayers. The psalmist said, "*If I regard iniquity in my heart, the Lord will not hear me*" (Ps. 66:18). Cherishing sin closes the ear of God. If you choose to disobey by not forgiving, God chooses not to listen when you pray. How many prayers are unanswered because of an unforgiving heart? If you have a track record of unanswered prayer, the first place to check is your unforgiveness list.

When unforgiveness is present, we do not sense God's presence. The psalmist said, "*In thy presence is fulness of joy*" (Ps. 16:11). God hides Himself when we wallow in pity, develop ingrown eyeballs, and harbor resentment. Focused on self, we lose all sense of God. As stated earlier, we are shut up in a spiritual vacuum. The absence of God's personal presence means we no longer experience joy.

Once I heard a story about an airplane that crashed on a snow-covered mountaintop. To survive, those still living began to cannibalize their fellow passengers who had perished in the crash. The tragedy is that nobody left the crash site. No one bothered to explore the other side of the mountain. If someone had, he would have discovered a bustling ski resort. The survivors all stayed at the crash site devouring the corpses of their fellow passengers. There they sat feeding on death instead of looking for a way of escape. We must leave the devastating places where we have been to find our way in the future. Feeding on dead things is no way to live! The point is that so often God's blessing is right in front of us. We experience His blessing when we turn our backs on resentments and other sins that hide His face. (This was a sermon illustration so I was unable to verify its accuracy.)

Again, as Nelson Mandela said, "Bitterness is the poison you drink that kills you before the other man dies." Bitterness not only kills the person who harbors it but also infects others with its deadly poison. The defiling fountain of bitterness is not content to remain alone; it seeps out and poisons everything it touches. Bitter preachers pollute congregations. The sins of the parents are often passed down to the children. When Christian leaders are mistreated, they must guard against bitterness. If not, their own offspring are likely to grow up despising God, the faith, and the church. When offended church members spill out their deadly poison at home, it is no wonder that their children are cynical and cold toward Christianity. We are exhorted, *"Follow peace with all men...lest any root of bitterness springing up trouble you, and thereby many be defiled"* (Heb. 12:14-15). The picture here is not of a placid pool but of a gushing, corrupt spring. Though some try to hold it in, the acid of bitterness is sure to eat through the container walls and contaminate others.

Indulging in the sin of unforgiveness not only puts a stumbling block before one's family but also offends unsaved and weaker Christians. Romans 14:13 warns against putting a stumbling block in someone else's path. It is better to suffer loss than to offend others. Jesus stated that it would be better to be thrown overboard into the ocean with a millstone about one's neck than to offend one of His little ones. (See Matthew 18:6.) Infecting a child with attitudes of hatred surely fits in the category of offending a little one. How many children have been hindered because of the stumbling block of unforgiveness?

Another destructive consequence of unforgiveness is emotional depression. Statistics tell us that many Americans suffer from this problem. Isolation during Covid lockdowns has caused mental health problems for many. Certainly, this condition can have a variety of causes. But who would deny that, in many cases, depression and anxiety are caused by pent-up hostility and unresolved hurt from broken relationships?

In contrast, the article "The Power of Forgiveness" by Lisa Collier Cool in the May 2004 issue of *Reader's Digest* suggests that forgiveness offers many health benefits. According to a study called "The Forgiveness Project," letting go of a grudge can slice one's stress level by up to 50 percent. Statistics also show that forgiveness improves our energy levels, moods, sleep patterns, and overall physical vitality. On the other hand, carrying around bitter and angry feelings is toxic to the body due to a release of the stress hormones adrenaline and cortisol. According to studies, brief releases of these hormones are harmless, but prolonged stress brought on by bitterness or anger turns these helpful hormones into toxins (Medicine, 2022).

The human spirit is our greatest asset when healthy but a handicap when broken. *"The spirit of a man will sustain his infirmity; but a wounded spirit who can bear?"* (Prov. 18:14). A damaged spirit is intolerable. Therefore, we must exercise the will to forgive when harsh blows fall.

A wounded spirit can be a debilitating force, especially when bitterness becomes an obsession. Detrimental side effects naturally follow in the wake of depression. Irrationality, the inability to think clearly, is a cognitive impairment that often results. The mind is short-circuited, and thinking processes become warped. Often the mind continually dwells on the same things. Over and over, the mind reviews the same trash. The problem can become so severe that one is totally incapacitated.

Improper relationships are also significant because of the unnecessary stress they bring. Tension, nervousness, and various types of mental illness are a few of the adverse results of disobedience in this area. The human body is not designed to house these repercussions. Praise the Lord for giving us clear steps for seeking to resolve conflicts.

In addition, unforgiveness has physical consequences. In a sermon, Rick Johnson once said, "Bitterness does more damage to the container in which it is stored than to the object on which it is poured." The human body cannot properly function with a spiritual cancer eating away at it. As we have seen, medical science claims that anger, bitterness, and hatred adversely affect the human body. Many illnesses, including heart disease, high blood pressure, ulcers, and a whole array of physical disorders, may be caused by this sin. It is only natural that a man's spiritual and emotional state should affect the health of his body. *"A merry heart doeth good like a medicine: but a broken spirit drieth the bones"* (Prov. 17:22).

When bitterness becomes a way of life instead of an isolated occurrence, it depletes the body. One physician told me that a lot of health complaints have spiritual roots. He began to prescribe my first book on forgiveness instead of treating symptoms with drugs. A free spirit and a joyful heart have a positive impact on physical health.

Dale Carnegie told the story of a grizzly bear in Yellowstone National Park. The bear was eating garbage someone had piled in a clearing. Probably the most ferocious animal in North America, the grizzly doesn't have many challengers. But while the bear was eating, a skunk appeared in the clearing and began eating too. Though the skunk rudely intruded, the bear didn't do anything, and they shared the food. Why? Because the bear knew the high cost of getting even!

Life is too short to live with the destructive consequences of unforgiveness. It's just not worth it. Obedience brings blessing, and one of life's greatest blessings is the inner healing forgiveness brings. Disobedience in this area, as in any other, carries a high price tag. Forgiveness is not a suggestion; it's a commandment. What's wonderful is that God never requires anything of us except what His grace enables us to do. The Lord never asks us to do anything without giving us the ability to carry out His directives. Because God requires forgiveness, failure to forgive brings negative consequences: *"Be not deceived; God is not mocked: for whatsoever a man soweth, that shall he also reap"* (Gal. 6:7). Aren't you glad for the grace of God, which enables us to forgive?

REFLECTIONS

1. "Bitterness is a poison you drink that kills you before the other man dies" (Mandela).

2. He who does not forgive destroys the bridge over which he himself must pass.

3. "Bitterness does more damage to the container in which it is stored than to the object on which it is poured" (Rick Johnson).

4. Life is too short to live with the destructive consequences of unforgiveness. It's just not worth it.

STUDY QUESTIONS AND POINTS OF APPLICATION

1. Briefly list the consequences of bitterness discussed in this chapter. After each, write down examples you have observed, either in your life or in the lives of others.

2. Use examples from the lives of others as a warning to avoid bitterness at all costs in your own life.

3. If you see evidences of bitterness in your own life, determine whether you have

repented of and made right the roots of your bitterness. If not, purpose to deal with them.

4. Praise the Lord for His grace that empowers us to forgive our offenders.

CHAPTER 4

HOW DOES UNFORGIVENESS GIVE GROUND TO SATAN?

Many Christians blame Satan for the breakdown of our culture. They decry the works of the devil through drugs, abortion, perversion, immorality, and a host of related evils. Yet Satan is perhaps gaining as much advantage through the unforgiving spirit of professing Christians as he is through all of these malignant vices combined. Satan knows men will sink deeply into the mire of overt sin on their own with little urging from him. But if he can defeat and mar the testimonies, health, and relationships of believers through unforgiveness, he will seize every opportunity he can. Paul warned the Corinthians how Satan gains an advantage over us through unforgiveness. (See 2 Corinthians 2:10-11.)

Relationships are the very crucible of life. They are among the most difficult yet enjoyable experiences we have. It is impossible to escape relationships. Because all of us are sinful by nature as well as by choice, it is only a matter of time before each relationship encounters a challenge. At times, we are deliberately offended. Other times, we are hurt and disappointed by the failure of the other party to meet our expectations.

All relationships tend to progress through at least four levels. Beginning a relationship with someone, we tend to see only the good and feel idealistic about the relationship. Soon, however, reality sets in, and we begin to wonder, *Hmmm, I didn't realize he was like that.* This level is quickly followed by feelings of resentment, a sense that we have been profoundly let down. We find ourselves disliking the way the other person is. If we are not careful, resentment sours into hatred and a desire to get out of the relationship altogether. But this exit may not be God's way.

When the issue of unforgiveness confronts us, we find ourselves acting like *pitchfork* Christians. We take our complaints and fling them over our shoulders, hoping so-and-so is listening and will get the point. But we must lay down our pitchforks, stop advertising our pain, and allow God's Word to penetrate us deeply. Failure to do so is costly. Refusing to forgive never ends well. It plunges us into a downward and spiritually destructive spiral.

Ephesians 4:31 details this harmful plummet. We must appreciate the context of this verse to grasp the gravity of the situation a lack of forgiveness generates. Ephesians 4:26-27 warns, *"Be ye angry, and sin not: let not the sun go down upon your wrath: Neither give place to the devil."*

Allowing the sun to go down on our wrath simply means that we harbor unforgiveness; we go to bed angry with someone. When that happens, we leave the door ajar for Satan. Ephesians 4:30 says we grieve God's Holy Spirit when we permit unforgiveness to fester. An unforgiving spirit is the devil's legal campground. It gives him a *place* of entry into our lives where he can war against us from within. Verse 31 describes the downward spiral: *"Let all bitterness, and wrath, and anger, and clamour, and evil speaking, be put away from you, with all malice."*

BITTERNESS

Carefully notice the phases of Satan's attack once we give him ground. His first tactic is that of poisoning. The word *bitterness* simply means *poison*. Bitterness is the direct result of an unforgiving spirit. A bitter person is someone who has been hurt. Someone has wounded him, neglected him, abused him, rejected him, slighted him, or cheated him—or, at least, he feels these hurts have happened to him. Rather than admitting the hurt and going to others to settle the matter, he harbors the hurt. Like a poison injected into the body, bitterness is a poison of the soul. The longer it stays, the more deeply entrenched it becomes, and the more it permeates the entire life.

The analogy of poison in the body is striking. Scripture refers to the *"gall of bitterness"* (Acts 8:23). Medical studies have demonstrated that bitterness of the soul is a factor in cholecystitis or gall bladder disease. Bitterness creates a chemical imbalance in the body, causing cholesterol to develop in the form of gallstones. The relationship is direct. Bitterness is an acid that eats away its own container.

Usually, bitterness is hidden under the surface. Hebrews 12:15 refers to it as a *root*. During biblical times, one of the shepherd's duties was to prepare a field for his sheep by carefully digging up any poisonous plants. Failure to do so resulted in sick or dead sheep. Likewise, we must *dig up* unforgiveness before it develops deep roots in our lives. *No one can harbor any degree of unforgiveness without becoming bitter.* Though we may mask bitterness before others and before ourselves, it is always destructive. Someone once said,

"Bitterness is like shooting yourself with a shotgun so the recoil will hit the other party!"

Bitterness shuts off the flow of God's life through our lives. Our prayers are hindered, and our lives become joyless and fruitless. One day, a mother disciplined her little girl. The angry girl knelt by her bed to say her prayers while her mother waited to tuck her in. The little girl prayed for her dad, her brothers, her sister, her aunts, her uncles, and her grandparents. After she said, "amen," she turned to her mother and announced, "I guess you noticed I left you out." The problem is, she had left God out too! Prayers from an unforgiving heart rise no higher than the ceiling. Praise and worship become a mockery, and life is poisoned at its source.

WRATH

Unresolved bitterness eventually leads to wrath, the next phase in this deadly spiral. Wrath, an interesting word, has the idea of heat connected to it. Wrath is that slow burn inside. It is an inward seething against the offender, a smoldering resentment. The word *resentment* means "to feel again." We delight to feel again the hurt and sorrow of wrongs done to us. Resentment provides a bittersweet pleasure. Wrath is the fire set by the initial hurt that was never resolved. It is akin to tossing rags into a trash can, setting them aflame, and placing the can in a closed closet. The rags burn slowly but surely.

Anger

When we fling the closed door open, the rags of smoldering wrath burst into flames. That picture describes anger, the third stage of Satan's assault on the unforgiving soul. When something happens to reveal the wrath and bitterness in someone's life, the person explodes in a fit of anger. Less-than-minor differences may develop into a full-scale war on a personal level. Such a display only reveals that a root of bitterness ignited the inferno.

Anger also carries the idea of something outward and open. Perhaps you have surprised yourself with an outburst of anger. You may not have realized how irritated or smoldering you were inside until an annoyance set you off. Your response was likely a root of bitterness displaying its fruit. We like to stonewall and wear a facade, pretending nothing is wrong. But it is impossible to purify the water by painting the pump. Bitterness eventually finds an outlet in anger.

Clamor

When anger bursts forth, it is frequently followed by clamor. You begin to verbalize. The word *clamor* itself suggests speech. Maybe you shout. Perhaps you argue at a high decibel, or you simply cry. The poison has so corrupted and filled your soul that it overflows through your tongue. The Bible describes such a tongue as *"a fire, a world of iniquity"* (James 3:6).

EVIL SPEAKING

Clamor turns to evil slander. You say words you never imagined you'd utter. "I hate you!" "I wish you were dead." "I'm sorry we ever had you for a child." "I hope I never see you again." Don't forget that often-repeated phrase, "I want a divorce." We say things we don't mean, all because of an unforgiving spirit, which arises out of a bitterness we never resolved. Someone once said, "Your venom poisons you more than your victim."

MALICE

Finally, evil speaking boils into malice. Malice is the desire to harm someone. Never be deceived about the depths to which Satan can take you when you yield him ground through failing to forgive. You may punch someone out. You may take a gun, knife, or another weapon and threaten him, or you may actually harm him. You may destroy someone financially. You may so maliciously slander him and assassinate his character that his reputation is ruined.

Satan is systematically demolishing the lives of many through their unforgiving spirit. Alexander Pope said, "Vice is a monster of so frightful mien, As, to be hated, needs but to be seen; Yet seen too oft, familiar with her face, We first endure, then pity, then embrace." Forgiveness is the basis of our relationship with God through Jesus Christ. Therefore, failing to forgive others is a serious sin, an affront to God. This sin will especially take us farther than we planned to go, keep us longer than we planned to stay, and cost us more than we planned to pay. We have only two outcomes. Either, by God's grace, we dig up the root of bitterness, or we allow it to ruin us.

REFLECTIONS

1. Bitterness will take you farther than you planned to go, keep you longer than you planned to stay, and cost you more than you planned to pay.

2. Bitterness is like a root. It lies beneath the surface. It is not easily detected.

3. Bitterness bears harmful fruit. Once Satan is given ground in the human heart, his influence spirals out of control.

4. *"Let all bitterness…be put away from you."* (See Ephesians 4:31-32.) Once you detect a root of bitterness and discern the fruit, you must give it the boot!

STUDY QUESTIONS AND POINTS OF APPLICATION

1. Unhealed hurts morph into bitterness. Unchecked bitterness gradually produces resentment against God. Can you recall Bible characters who became bitter?

2. The children of Israel came to the bitter waters at Marah. To heal the bitter waters, God instructed Moses to cut down a tree and cast it into that polluted pool. The only tree that can heal the bitter waters in the human heart is a tree called Calvary!

3. Carefully read Ephesians 4:26-32. Take note of the downward steps through which Satan leads someone who has failed to forgive. Are you experiencing any of these steps in your life because of your unforgiveness?

   If so, recall the author's statement that forgiveness is a deliberate choice of the mind and will. Realize that you have yielded ground to Satan. Confess your sin to God and ask for His forgiveness. Pray in the name and through the blood of Jesus Christ that God will restore to you the ground you have given to Satan.

CHAPTER 5

You've Convinced Me— But Where Do I Start?

The Bible provides crystal-clear guidelines for most situations and principles that cover every situation. Individual circumstances determine the proper approach. When an obvious offense has occurred, then *"go"* and *"be reconciled"* (Matt. 5:24). In these situations, God calls us to be peacemakers, to go in lowliness with the intent to restore. The proper way is to take the blame for *our* wrong actions, reactions, or attitudes. This is not the time to attack the other party. An individual's response is between that person and God. Our need is to take responsibility for our offenses. Sometimes, we simply need *"to go."* (We will learn more about this stage in Section 2: "Seeking Forgiveness.")

Then, there are times when we must forgive. Jesus said in Mark 11:25, *"And when ye stand praying, forgive, if ye have ought against any: that your Father also…may forgive you your trespasses."* This forgiveness includes those fleshly acts that are sure to arise in all of us sooner or later. We don't need to go running to everyone about every little thing. When minor offenses occur, simply make a choice to release that debt and get on with your praying. Someone once said, "Forgiveness is absorbing the liability someone else deserves to pay." Don't get bogged down in trivial offenses. Grow up in Christ! Deal with the matter in your heart and move on.

When I began a serious study of forgiveness in preparation for a sermon, God began to speak to my heart. Honestly, I was unaware of the bitterness and resentment in my own soul. However, anxiety and a lack of peace caused me to realize something was wrong. The longer I studied, the more convicted I became.

One day, I took a walk in our backyard. I decided that the time had come to take action and make some hard decisions. Out of desperation, I prayed spontaneously in a way I had never prayed before. "Lord," I said, "I am choosing right now to forgive the person who embarrassed me in front of my friends when I was a child. It hurt, Lord, but I release him from that debt…. Lord, my friend hurt me and caused me trouble by breaking my confidence. I am making a decision right now to release him from that debt…. Lord, there are some people who lied to me. The lie hurt, but I choose now to forgive them. I'll never hold the offense against them again." It took me thirty minutes to shred my You-owe-me list. When I released those people, God released me, and I left my backyard with the joy of the Lord in my heart again.

I recall another case when a lady had been offended by a former pastor. He was unaware of his offense. But God spoke to the lady about the unforgiveness in her heart. She chose to forgive her former pastor for the offense. Later that night, she called him and told him that she had forgiven him. Remember, he was unaware of any offense on his part. He did not respond positively.

In cases like this when we need to forgive, it is *not* always necessary to inform the party who caused the offense of our decision. If he is not asking for forgiveness, we should keep the matter between ourselves and God. If he is unrepentant, telling him we have forgiven him won't do any good. Remember Jesus' example when He prayed, *"Father, forgive them…"* (Luke 23:34). He kept the matter between Him and His Heavenly Father. Jesus said nothing to those who abused Him, crucified Him, and forsook Him. He dealt exclusively with His Father.

In the event that you cannot settle an offense in your heart, you may need to approach the other party. When dealing with Christians, Matthew 18 gives us the procedure to follow when we have been offended and when gracious confrontation is required: *"Moreover if thy brother shall trespass against thee, go and tell him his fault between thee and him alone: if he shall hear thee, thou hast gained thy brother"* (Matt. 18:15-17). There are more steps to follow should approaching your offender prove to be unsuccessful.

When we are offended, notice that the Bible says we are to go to *"him alone."* (See Matthew 18:15.) Don't speak to another soul; approach your offender directly. Isn't that hard to do? Someone has said, "Your tongue is in a wet place, and it's easy for it to slip!" Something on the inside, the flesh, wants to broadcast our hurt to everyone. Obedience to this principle is essential if we are to avoid causing others to take up offense on our behalf against those who have wronged us. Much division can be avoided by speaking about the offense only to our offender and not to anyone else. How we need the Holy Spirit's control to keep our tongues in check by speaking only to the one who has wronged us.

Sometimes, we need to go; other times, we need to forgive; but *most often, we need God to forgive us.*

Suppose you have entertained negative thoughts about someone. That person hasn't really offended you and is unaware of your thoughts. If he hasn't done anything wrong and doesn't realize that you have erected mental barriers against him, you don't need to go to him. But you *do* need to go to God and ask for His forgiveness. Never go to someone in your church and say, "You aren't aware of it, but I have had evil thoughts about you. Would you please forgive me for thinking that you are the biggest jerk in the whole congregation?" That type of confession is never warranted.

Likewise, we should confess lustful thoughts about someone to God alone. Never say, "I have had lustful thoughts about you, and I want you to forgive me." You should approach the other party *only* if he or she knows about the problem. Sharing unknown thoughts or feelings may create thoughts in the other party's mind that were not there previously. Expressing lustful thoughts openly may also arouse the same thoughts in someone else and precipitate an immoral relationship. Also never say to someone, "I have disliked you." This type of confession can create more problems, for example, resentment. When others are unaware and not offended, we should seek forgiveness solely from God since our sin is between us and Him alone.

We also need to grant forgiveness when others come to us and seek to right a wrong. Verbally expressing forgiveness is extremely important. When someone approaches us and apologizes, we should never say, "Oh, forget it" or "That's all right. It doesn't matter." The appropriate response is "I forgive you." Those three words are what a guilty conscience needs to hear. Our response should be a means of release to our offender. When someone asks us for forgiveness, we should never be bashful about saying, "I forgive you."

REFLECTIONS

1. Sometimes, we need to go and seek reconciliation. Many times, we just need to forgive. But most often, we need to ask God to forgive us.

2. Forgiveness is absorbing the liability someone else deserves to pay.

3. Jesus worked out forgiveness between the Father and Him. He did not say a word to His unrepentant abusers.

4. Be very cautious about telling someone you are forgiving them if they are not requesting forgiveness.

STUDY QUESTIONS AND POINTS OF APPLICATION

1. Why is obedience to God's directive to talk to an offender alone so important?

2. What are two situations when we should seek forgiveness only from the Lord without mentioning it to anyone else?

3. Are you aware of instances where you just need to let something go?

4. What is the appropriate biblical response when someone seeks your forgiveness?

CHAPTER 6

WHY IS IT SO HARD TO FORGIVE?

Years ago, the Lord enabled me to adopt what I call my *up-front policy*. Harboring bitterness, resentment, and unresolved conflicts had brought me to a state of inner hostility and bondage. I was tired of being lied to and taken advantage of, but confrontation wasn't my way. I didn't enjoy it at all! Why was I reluctant to approach others when they had offended me? What was the real reason behind my timidity?

"Only by pride cometh contention" (Prov. 13:10). I'll never forget the night God opened my heart to this verse and convicted me of pride. The distance was growing between one of my closest friends and me. *Little*

things were piling up and putting a wedge between us. Differences had led to conflicts that I needed to resolve, if the friendship was to continue. God showed me that the contention between my friend and me was the result of pride—*my* pride!

First, I was afraid to confront my friend because I *feared rejection.* If I told him what I honestly thought, I knew there was the possibility that he wouldn't accept me. Could our friendship withstand total honesty? I wasn't sure. Since then, I have learned that no one can maintain real friendship apart from honesty and transparency. The possibility of losing a good friend posed an ominous threat to my pride. Fearing rejection, I kept quiet.

Second, pride caused me to respond to my friend's faults and inconsistencies with a *critical spirit* instead of with godly concern. Pride eliminates compassion and gives rise to criticism instead. Critical and contentious attitudes indicate a root of pride. The only way to look down on someone is to assume you are better than he is. A humble person recognizes he has faults and is capable of the worst. But a proud person sets himself up as a judge and finds a multitude of reasons to condemn, many of which may be accurate. The real problem is not recognizing the other person's faults but the way we respond to those faults. Instead of praying for my friend, I had harbored resentment, which became increasingly easy.

Someone once said, "Where Satan can't go personally, he just sends a critic!" The Bible refers to Satan as an *accuser.* (See Revelation 12:10.) In the Garden of Eden, he accused God of lying: *"And the serpent said unto the woman, Ye shall not surely die: For God doth know that in the day ye eat thereof, then your eyes shall be opened, and ye shall be as gods, knowing good and evil"* (Gen. 3:4-5). Here Satan contradicted what God had said and accused Him of concealing the truth from Adam and Eve. Satan not only slanders God but also accuses man:

> *And the Lord said unto Satan, Whence comest thou? Then Satan answered the Lord, and said, From going to and fro in the earth, and from walking up and down in it. And the Lord said unto Satan, Hast thou considered my servant Job, that there is none like him in the earth, a perfect and an upright man, one that feareth God, and escheweth evil? Then Satan answered the Lord, and said, Doth Job fear God for nought? Hast not thou made an hedge about him, and about his house, and about all that he hath on every side? thou hast blessed the work of his hands, and his*

THE POWER OF FORGIVENESS

substance is increased in the land. But put forth thine hand now, and touch all that he hath, and he will curse thee to thy face (Job 1:7-11).

In Genesis, Satan accused God to man; in Job, he accused man to God. How similar we are to Satan when we slander and criticize!

A compassionate soul will be broken, not bitter, over his brother's sins. Pride is the source of a critical, unforgiving spirit. The lack of concerned confrontation only intensifies the problem.

Third, my pride would not allow me to approach my friend because the confrontation would only *expose my own needs*. I did not want my friend to know that such trivial matters bothered me. If I was honest, I would unveil my own weakness and wickedness. Pride will cost us friendships that are some of life's most valuable treasures. Pride can cause us to be quiet to save face, rather than risk being laid bare by confronting the problem.

When the Holy Spirit showed me my pride, I knew the only way to crush it was to do the thing I feared most. I needed to go to my brother in lowliness and admit that the friction in our relationship was due to my pride. After taking the low road and acknowledging my faults, I was able to share honest concerns. This is what real friendships are made of: truthfulness. At this point, I decided to be up-front all the time.

When you experience a misunderstanding or feel slighted by your friend, your best plan is to put your cards on the table. Approach the other party calmly and truthfully. Many times, the other party may be oblivious to what seems obvious to you. Resolve the problem as soon as you can. Don't wait until your stomach is twisted into knots. Why not adopt your own *up-front policy* now?

We often withhold forgiveness for reasons other than pride. One reason is selfishness. We have been hurt. We didn't deserve that unfair treatment. Things didn't go as we had planned. By nature, we all have a *god complex.* For some reason, we believe that we are entitled to preferential treatment. We think we have a right to be respected and treated well. In fact, our self-centeredness is so intense that our primary concern is our own rights and feelings. Once offended, we tend to live in an emotional prison because our expectations have not been met. Jesus invited His followers to take up their cross, an instrument of death, and follow Him. (See Matthew 16:24.) He asked them to die to their own way. Taking up the cross was a picture of surrendered rights and expectations. Do you need to surrender your rights to God?

If your own self-centeredness is holding you back from making the right choices, you could choose to forgive. Perhaps you are willing to forgive if your offender will only *fess up*. But you don't need to wait for an apology to forgive others. When Stephen was being stoned, he uttered a prayer on behalf of those who were stoning him: *"And he kneeled down, and cried with a loud voice, Lord, lay not this sin to their charge"* (Acts 7:60). We are obligated to forgive regardless of what others do or don't do. There's no need to wait; go ahead and forgive. Pride and selfishness, two of Satan's main character traits, are also two of the leading hindrances to forgiveness. Do you need to *"take up* [your] *cross"* (Matt. 16:24) and put this deadly duo to death?

Another hindrance to freedom is pain. Some experiences hurt so badly that many dread bringing up those painful emotions. This is especially true when some have tried to simply ignore those memories or bury them by denial.

One woman said tearfully, "My father is ninety years old and is lying on his deathbed. When I was a little girl, my father did terrible things to me. I just made a decision to forgive him for all those horrible things he did to me." It was painful but necessary for this woman to face the hurts she had carried for more than fifty years. Incest, rape, child abuse, and other offenses are so unpleasant that people will run instead of deal with them. Denial is a coping mechanism. But, in such cases, healing may come only when those who are hurt are willing to confront and work through forgiveness.

It was not easy for a young woman to forgive the man who had molested her when she was a teenager. The experience was painful, but her conscience was convicted. She knew she was obligated to forgive the man of his awful crime. With tears, a trembling voice, and a bent knee, she prayed, "Lord, I am making a decision to forgive that man who took advantage of me as a teenager." As painful as the experience was, forgiveness was the only way for her to recover from this life-shattering experience. Spiritual surgery may hurt, but it alone can bring healing. Whatever scar it may leave will be easier to handle than the gaping wound you now bear.

Consider the example of a woman who was abducted from a Florida parking lot. While her three children watched, three men threw her into a van and drove away. They inflicted on her every imaginable cruelty and perversion. They burned her. They even took a knife and flayed her face and body before leaving her on the ground to die. If not for the cold temperatures that clotted her blood, she would have bled to death. Crawling two miles to the highway, she was so mutilated that those who helped her couldn't tell if she was a man or a woman. Later, the authorities caught the men and sentenced them to life in prison.

After their trial, reporters asked the woman if she could forgive her abductors. She replied, "I am a Christian, and my faith commands me to forgive them. They took one day of my life, and I am not going to give them another one." What a testimony of forgiveness! Someone has wisely said, "Forgiveness never justifies the sins of others, but it keeps their sins from defeating us."

In cases of moral evil, God has ordained the government to punish evildoers. Scripture teaches that civil authorities should punish such crimes. Within some groups, there is a great misunderstanding concerning civil government's responsibility. *"For he is the minister of God to thee for good. But if thou do that which is evil, be afraid; for he beareth not the sword in vain: for he is the minister of God, a revenger to execute wrath upon him that doeth evil"* (Rom. 13:4).

Never confuse the Christian's responsibility to forgive with the responsibility of the legal system to punish criminals. When a crime has been committed, we do not have the right to pardon. Granting pardon is the right of the court of law, which God has established as His minister for the purpose of avenging wrong. The government must punish crime. We, as believers, must forgive those who offend us. Justice is the duty of the judiciary; forgiveness is our duty.

REFLECTIONS

1. Conflict is the consequence of pride and self-centeredness. Confronting problems is not pleasant, but it is necessary.

2. Fear of rejection, a critical spirit, and fear of exposure will hinder us from restoring faltering relationships. All three of these hindrances find their source in pride.

3. Satan's title, *diabolos,* means slanderer or accuser. Where Satan does not go personally, he sends a critic.

4. Forgiveness never justifies the sins of others, but it keeps their sins from defeating us.

STUDY QUESTIONS AND POINTS OF APPLICATION

1. Consider the three major reasons forgiving others is often difficult. Which reason(s) has God spoken to you about personally?

2. Satan is referred to as the *"accuser of* [the] *brethren."* (See Revelation 12:10.) Rehearse scriptural examples of Satan's accusations.

3. Forgiveness can be granted in the absence of an apology. In the Bible, who chose to forgive when there was no acknowledgment of wrongdoing?

4. What is the difference between pardon and forgiveness? Who has the responsibility for each of these?

CHAPTER 7

WHAT SHOULD I DO WHEN I'M TEMPTED TO UNFORGIVE?

Once we have chosen to forgive, we must continue to choose the freedom of forgiveness. A decision to forgive is no guarantee that bitter thoughts and emotions will never return. It is only normal that deep wounds leave emotional scars. We shouldn't think it strange when thoughts and feelings of hurt arise. That is normal. It is time now to learn to change our thinking and emotions. Otherwise, we may feel tempted to *unforgive* the person we forgave. Here are some helpful rules:

Rule #1. Don't rehearse the details once the debt has been canceled.

One man told his friend, "Every time my wife and I get in an argument, she gets historical." His friend asked, "You mean *hysterical?*"

"No, I mean *historical,*" the man said. "She brings up everything I've ever done and just keeps bringing it back up."

When you have chosen to forgive, reviewing painful circumstances and events in your mind will do no good. Dwelling on some aspect of the offense will only cause you to fume. Don't let the Enemy bombard you with recurring episodes of the same old story after you have closed the book. Stop playing the offensive episode in the theater of your mind.

Hurtful thoughts will return but you must choose not to mentally review them. You do not need to allow a dwelling place for every thought that comes floating through your mind. Just as you have decided to forgive, you must choose again and again not to review the story. Don't rehearse it! Someone once said, "It is impossible to absolutely forget in the sense that it [the offense] will never come to mind. But the times that the offense does come to mind will lessen as time goes on."

Philippians 3:13 says, "…*forgetting those things which are behind, and reaching forth unto those things which are before.*" We tend to remember the things we should forget and to forget the things we should remember. But we can purposely choose to forget. We can choose to neglect hurtful memories and put them out of our minds. Forgiveness means we intentionally stop visiting the corridors in our minds that we have already been down so many times. We've been down those hallways many times. We know that there is no solution there. So there is no use continuing to go down them!

One day, two Christian men were enjoying fellowship. When one man reminded his friend of an unpleasant experience, the friend replied, "Yes, I distinctly remember forgetting that!"

Rule #2. Don't nurse the hurt.

"I really was taken advantage of," you say. Hold everything! Now is not the time to have a pity party. Justifying yourself and building a case for your innocence are steps that are no longer necessary. You have released the offending party from his debts. He owes you nothing. The matter is now between him and God. Do not take back the right to justice that you have given to God. As a Christian, you have already surrendered your rights anyhow.

Sam Jones, an evangelist, had difficulty forgiving others the wrongs done to him. But one day, he made a decision. "I thought of the grace of God," he said, "and then made up my mind that I was not going to fall out with anybody until that person treated me worse than I had treated Jesus."

Yes, you were hurt; you were wronged; and you were offended. But now that you have forgiven, you dare not indulge in feeling sorry for yourself. Don't nurse your hurt!

RULE #3. DON'T CURSE THE OFFENDER.

Vengeance isn't ours; it belongs to God. Never allow room for wicked thoughts of revenge toward an offender. "But he really deserves…" Wait a minute! What he deserves is irrelevant. That matter is out of our hands. The Lord will do as He sees fit. It is not for us to wish or pray for evil on the person who has hurt us. Jesus said, *"Love your enemies, bless them that curse you, do good to them that hate you, and pray for them which despitefully use you, and persecute you"* (Matt. 5:44). Notice the words *"love," "bless," "do good,"* and *"pray."* These are the only ways we can maintain a proper attitude. By an act of the will, we have granted forgiveness. Likewise, by continual acts of love and prayer, we will obtain and maintain a proper attitude of heart.

Rule #4. Do pray for the offender.

Here is the secret of staying free from bitterness. Do you remember Job? He was stripped of his possessions, children, and health. Then his three friends accused and blamed him for all of his troubles. They were confident that his sin had landed him in his awful plight. When they accused him, Job responded by praying for them! *"And the Lord turned the captivity of Job, when he prayed for his friends"* (Job 42:10). God released Job from bondage when he prayed for his friends, even though they weren't exactly the type of friends you would feel like praying for. Praying for offenders is the secret of staying free.

Two Christian friends embarked on a business agreement they believed would benefit both of them. One, a mechanic, agreed to work on his friend's car. When the car owner lost a lot of money because of faulty work, he confronted his mechanic friend. But the mechanic refused to acknowledge his fault and to compensate his friend. Immediately, a wall shot up between the two men. The car owner felt cheated. The offensive episode replayed in his mind time and again, and he felt uncomfortable whenever he saw the other man. Anger welled up each time they met.

Despite his feelings, the offended brother tried to be cordial because he knew that was the Christian thing to do! Can you identify with this scenario? We all can. What happened? The car owner who was taken advantage of decided to forgive his brother. Even so, angry feelings returned, and he tried his best to be free of them. Finally, he began praying for his mechanic friend, asking God to bless him. Every time the offense came to mind, he prayed. It didn't take long for his negative emotional response to disappear.

It is impossible to harbor resentment toward someone when you pray for that person consistently. Each time anger toward the offender returns, pray for him immediately. Ask God's blessing on him and his family. Believe me, you can't remain bitter when you are praying for someone. Every time angry thoughts return, engage in prayer. God will transform your attitude and disposition as you pray for your offender. In time, your anger and emotional hostility will fade, and God will replace them with genuine love. Sometimes you may even find pity in your heart for the person who hurt you. Making the right choices will keep you free from anger that enslaves.

Others may not get along with you, but you can do your part to get along with them. When you respond to others properly, you are obeying God and He will share His peace with you. Reconciliation, restitution, and forgiveness are ways God deals with offenses.

What steps must you take to reach the happy place where your heart and conscience are free?

REFLECTIONS

1. A decision to forgive is no guarantee that bitter thoughts and emotions will never return.

2. We tend to remember the things we should forget and forget the things we should remember. We must purposely choose to forget.

3. "*...forgetting those things which are behind...*" (Phil. 3:13). The word *forget* means "to neglect or ignore." Hurtful memories must be put out of our minds by refusing to rehearse them.

4. Words to ponder: "I...made up my mind that I was not going to fall out with anybody until that person treated me worse than I had treated Jesus."

STUDY QUESTIONS AND POINTS OF APPLICATION

1. "Once I have forgiven my offender, the problem is over and I can rest assured that it will never bother me again." Is this statement true or false? Explain your answer.

2. List four practical steps you can take to avoid negative emotional responses once you have forgiven your offender(s).

3. If needed, apply these rules now. Invest some moments praying for those who have hurt you.

4. Purpose in your heart to follow those steps. Ask God to remind you of those steps when you are tempted to unforgive.

PRACTICAL STEPS TO FORGIVING OTHERS

Here is a summary of what we have learned in Section 1. This review is provided to help you make a thorough application by granting forgiveness to those who have offended you.

1. Understand that forgiveness is not…
    - Denying your pain,
    - Deleting painful experiences from your memory,
    - Working up a feeling or a positive emotion,

- Asking God to forgive you for being angry with the person who offended you,

- Asking God to pardon the person who hurt you,

- Justifying or understanding why your offender acted toward you as he did.

2. Understand that forgiveness is...

   - A commandment and not a suggestion,

   - A decision and not a feeling,

   - Canceling the debt and expecting nothing in return,

   - A choice, an act of your will.

3. Get alone with God. List those who have offended you and the events for which you need to forgive them.

4. Ask God to forgive you for your bitterness toward your offender(s).

5. Pray through your list aloud. Deal with each situation individually. Pray something like this: "Lord, I was hurt and I am angry. But I am choosing right now to forgive _____ for _____. I release him for hurting me and will never hold the

offense against him again. It's out of my hands. From now on, it's between You and him. I release the debt." Go through your entire list. When you have finished, tear up your You-owe-me list!

6.   Thank the Lord for using this difficult situation to conform you into the image of His Son.

7.   Understand that unless the other party has sought your forgiveness, informing the other party that you have forgiven him is often unwise.

8.   When bitter thoughts and hostile feelings return, immediately pray for those who have hurt you.

SEEKING
FORGIVENESS

CHAPTER 8

IS IT REALLY NECESSARY TO ASK FOR FORGIVENESS?

Once you have forgiven others their wrongs, you are ready to move on to the second half of forgiveness. After you have granted forgiveness to those who have wronged you, you must seek forgiveness from those you have wronged. Believers should seek forgiveness for their wrongs from both God *and* man. While the previous section touched on this matter, it is essential to take the necessary steps to clear your conscience.

First, you need to go to the Lord, if you haven't already, and confess your sins. Our relationship with God is affected by our many horizontal relationships. If you have sinned against others by being unforgiving, you have also sinned against the Lord. You need to confess this sin. The Bible says, *"If we confess our sins* [agree with God about them], *he is faithful and just to forgive us our sins, and to cleanse us from all unrighteousness"* (1 John 1:9). To walk with God, we must *agree with God*. The moment we become aware of wrong actions, attitudes, or reactions, we should *side with God* and own up. Agreeing with God means that we take the witness stand against ourselves. Confession is the first step.

Next, you may need to ask for forgiveness and make restitution.

"I'm not used to talking to you face to face; I normally talk behind your back. Will you forgive me?" One woman tearfully said these words while standing in front of her fellow church members. Was her request for forgiveness appropriate? In her case, yes. She had publicly sinned with her tongue by gossiping, and the entire church was aware of her sin. In this instance, and many others like it, we need to seek forgiveness from those we have wronged.

Let's examine instances in which we have wronged another party. Once we are convinced of our offense toward someone, we need to go to that person and seek reconciliation. The Holy Spirit's mission is the conviction of sin. When the Spirit broods over someone, the person becomes aware of things previously unnoticed.

A bakery worker felt convicted about two bags of cookies he had stolen. Stealing was an offense that resulted in automatic firing. He was so desperate to get a clear conscience that he confessed his sin to his boss. He was not worried about the possible consequences. He was desperate to clear his conscience. His employer was shocked; no one had ever admitted to thievery and asked for forgiveness. (By the way, the bakery worker didn't lose his job.) Afterward, he joyfully testified to the newfound freedom resulting from clearing his conscience.

A seminary president was surprised when a graduate returned his diploma and admitted to cheating on an exam. In the middle of a church business meeting, a man rose to his feet and said, "I was not wrong in what I said a moment ago, but I sure was wrong in the way I said it. Will you forgive me?" Can you imagine the surprise of the IRS employee who opened an envelope and found a check and a letter from someone who was admitting to cheating on his taxes? What about the young man who apologized to his parents for being disrespectful and rebellious? A common thread runs through all of these cases; in every one of them, the individual was seeking to clear his conscience. When the Holy Spirit brings conviction, a guilty conscience becomes unbearable. Instances like these are common in seasons of revival. When God makes us aware of wrongs, we must respond in obedience. If we don't, we develop a hardened conscience.

In the first grade, some of my classmates and I teamed up to steal items from a small country store. One of us would distract the widow storekeeper who ran this particular Esso station. While distracted, another one of us would sneak behind the counter and lift cigarettes and Esso Tiger keychains. (I bet I collected one hundred of these keyrings!) I was not bothered about it until I became a Christian. Then my conscience began to trouble me. I went to that widow store owner and asked forgiveness. She brushed it off, "Harold, all children take things." I said, "I don't know what other children do, but this child [me] was wrong and I am sorry." It was not a big deal for her, but it was huge to me. There were several people with whom I had to clear things up. As I obeyed in the matter of restitution, it was like weights being lifted off my shoulders. The peace and freedom that followed were incredible!

Like a tall building, life's foundations must be deep, strong, and secure. Confession, forgiveness, and restitution are foundational principles for obedient, successful Christian living. We are responsible for the day-by-day, hour-by-hour, moment-by-moment task of appropriating these indispensable principles as the need arises. As long as we are living on planet Earth, we will need to apply God's rules to human relationships. These truths relate to the home, church, work, and neighborhood. By responding in total obedience, we can do our part in maintaining a clear conscience. Life is too short to carry this baggage. This is the right way to live!

REFLECTIONS

1. I do not have a license to wrong those who have wronged me. My wrong reaction is sin, which needs to be put right with God.

2. Confession is my responsibility toward God. Making restitution is my obligation to those I have wronged.

3. Obtaining and maintaining a clear conscience are key to personal peace and spiritual freedom.

4. When God convicts us, we must respond in obedience.

STUDY QUESTIONS AND POINTS OF APPLICATION

1. Walking with God requires a harmonious relationship. What does confession mean?

2. Keeping in step with God makes us sensitive to offenses we commit toward others. Spiritual dullness and insensitivity result from ignoring such offenses or failing to clear our conscience. Can you think of someone who could face you right now and say, "You hurt me and never tried to set things right"?

3. If someone, possibly several people, come to mind, purpose before God to obey Him as He directs you through the truths presented in this section of the book.

CHAPTER 9

BUT WHAT IF...?

A host of excuses may flood the mind of the one seeking forgiveness. Since this act of obedience is of such vital importance, we should not be surprised that Satan will seek to cloud the issue. We should regard excuses as satanic obstacles. Once convicted, the child of God must hurdle all obstacles hindering him from seeking forgiveness and must recognize those warped reasonings for what they are: assaults of the evil one. Do any of these excuses sound familiar?

"It happened before I got saved." Once we are converted, God has forgiven our sins. But His forgiveness doesn't excuse us from our responsibility to make things right. In Luke 19, Zacchaeus repaid those whom he had cheated, even though he had committed those wrongs before his conversion. I believe one clear evidence of genuine salvation is the overwhelming impulse to put our wrongs right. The cross points in two directions: heavenward and earthward, that is, vertical and horizontal. It points toward the Lord and our fellow man. And the implications affect our dealings with others.

Paul testified, *"And herein do I exercise myself, to have always a conscience void of offence toward God, and **toward** men"* (Acts 24:16, emphasis added). The apostle worked at keeping himself in the clear with the Lord and his fellow men. Once he came to the Lord, Zacchaeus knew wrongs needed to be put right. So he repaid those whom he had wronged.

You may be thinking to yourself, *I don't have enough years left in my life to seek forgiveness from all the people I have wronged!* The Lord will point out those cases in which you need to act. Don't feel overwhelmed. What you need to be concerned about now is your willingness to obey God in everything He reveals. God will guide you along the way.

"I've lost track of those people. They have moved." A man stood up in church and described a most unusual answer to prayer. When he was a teenager, he had stolen money from the service station where he worked. Now middle-aged, he told the Lord he would clear up his offense if he saw his old boss. The service station owner had moved, and the man hadn't seen him in decades. Guess who he saw at the bank the day after he prayed that prayer? The service station owner! What a glowing testimony of obedience the man gave that night! The boss was a Christian and what a time of rejoicing they had in the bank parking lot.

When our attempt to locate an offended party fails, we have another way to resolve the matter. During her high school years, a woman stole from the department store where she worked. The store had since closed, and she had no idea where the owner lived. I counseled her to pray about the situation and to tell the Lord she was willing to clear up the matter if she and the store owner ever crossed paths. Meanwhile, I suggested that she give to her church a sum of money equivalent to what she had stolen. Having done all in her power to pay back the stolen money, she could honestly say she had sought forgiveness. She no longer needed to feel guilty about her past offense.

"It was so small." If the offense is big enough to bother you, that's a good sign that you need to deal with it. Office supplies you took, half-truths you told, *unChristlike* ways you responded—you need to act on these and other *small* offenses.

THE POWER OF FORGIVENESS

My wife was expecting our first child when we drove from Flagstaff to see the Grand Canyon one morning. En route to the canyon, we visited the Sun Crater Volcano Park. Lava rocks were everywhere inside the park. I hopped out of the car and picked up two stones to show my wife. Her response was, "What are you doing with those rocks?" My response was, "I'm taking them home as souvenirs."

Immediately she said, "Did you see that sign?"

And I said, "What sign?"

The truth is, I saw the sign that said, "Please do *not* remove anything from the park." But I only read enough of the sign to know what the rest of the sign was saying! Since I did not want to abide by the policy, I stopped reading. My wife informed me about the prohibition.

Then I said, "It's only a couple of rocks."

She said, "What if everybody took a couple of rocks?"

I replied, "Look around...if everybody took two rocks it would take millions of years to exhaust the supply!" Then I grabbed the rocks and stuffed them under the seat.

Needless to say, the atmosphere was tense, and I failed to appreciate the beauty of the canyon that day.

I had violated my conscience. At length, I forgot all about it. But when we arrived back home, I was ill at ease. Peace had left my soul. I was nervous and cranky. After a couple of miserable days, I prayed, "Lord, what's wrong?" Immediately it flashed into my mind: "Those rocks!" Promptly I retrieved the rocks and packaged them to mail back. I composed a letter to the park ranger: "Recently I visited your park, and I stole these rocks. I am returning them and asking your forgiveness for stealing these rocks."

Hurriedly, I drove to the post office. Thoughts invaded my mind, thoughts like, *You are nuts. Nobody does things like this. If you send these rocks back, a van will pull up in the driveway and guys in white suits will haul you off to the psych ward.* But I disregarded those thoughts. The moment I paid the postage, peace flooded my soul. I was *free*!

By taking care of small things, you narrow the likelihood of overlooking bigger things. Wrong is wrong, whether big or small. I had rather go too far in matters like this than justify sin of any size or sort.

"I'm too sensitive." Better to be *too* sensitive than to be calloused with a seared conscience. If you are too sensitive, the Lord can change you. But violating your conscience through disobedience is a serious matter. Hardening your conscience will render you unable to hear God's voice, and you may find yourself rationalizing, excusing, and overlooking larger problems.

"I can't afford it; money is involved." Picture this scenario: a Canadian couple sat in their pastor's office. The man was terribly distressed, and the wife feared her husband was going to be "too honest." Breaking down and pouring out his soul, the man said that he and his wife had purchased camera equipment in the United States and brought it back to Canada without paying tax. The pastor phoned the border agency and explained the situation. The wife wept, fearing her husband would go to jail. The border agent simply told them how much tax to pay. Because of fear, this dear woman had complicated what turned out to be a simple solution. The Lord knows about your finances; He can meet your needs. Don't allow the excuse of finances to sidetrack your obedience to God.

"They will not understand." You may be surprised by how much those who were offended will understand. Most people are so taken aback by the honesty that they not only understand but also gladly forgive. In the vast majority of cases I've witnessed, the response has been positive.

But remember, the offended person's response is not the most important issue. You have no guarantee that the other party will react positively. Your goal is to obey God by clearing your conscience. All God asks is that you obey. Whether the other person accepts your forgiveness is between him and God. Once you do your part, you are clear. Possible outcomes are not the determining factor. Obedience on your part is the most important thing.

REFLECTIONS

1. Zacchaeus repaid those he had cheated before his conversion. One mark of saving grace is taking responsibility for wrongs and putting them right.

2. There is no such thing as a small sin because there is no small God to sin against.

3. Satan is not only an accuser, he's also a master excuser. He offers all manner of reasons to disobey God.

4. Someone has suggested that an excuse is "the skin of a reason stuffed with a lie." Satan, the father of lies, will do all in his power to thwart or delay obedience in this crucial matter of clearing the conscience.

STUDY QUESTIONS AND POINTS OF APPLICATION

1. Take a moment to list the six excuses detailed in this chapter. Are you using any of these excuses to avoid obeying God by seeking forgiveness?

2. What should you do if, after prayer, you are unable to locate the party to whom you need to make restitution?

3. If you are aware of a situation involving the need to make financial restitution, use a concordance and locate Scripture passages that give principles concerning proper repayment. You can find these in both the Old and New Testaments. Determine before God what He would have you do in your particular case and trust Him to enable you to do it.

4. Reject any excuses and seek God's grace to obey Him fully.

HOW CAN I TELL IF MY CONSCIENCE IS VIOLATED?

Many New Testament references to the conscience indicate its importance. The purpose of God's commands is to produce a pure and loving heart, a sincere faith, and a good conscience. (See 1 Timothy 1:5.) Once the conscience is offended, serious repercussions result. See if you can identify with any of these indications of a violated conscience.

Uncontrollable Anger:

When certain people or subjects come up in conversation, you tend to strike out in anger. You "can't stand" to hear good things about certain people. When the person's name is mentioned, it reignites hostile feelings. Should thoughts about that person enter your mind, your pulse races. You can't explain it, but you are unable to control your feelings. Inside you feel like you are about to explode. Others sense your frustration. The longer you dwell on your hurt, the more the tension mounts.

Nathan the prophet confronted David. He told the king about a wealthy man who had confiscated the sole prized possession of a peasant. While possessing countless animals, the rich man took the poor man's pet lamb and made a meal with it for a traveler. When David heard this story, he exploded with rage, *"The man that hath done this **thing** shall surely die"* (2 Sam. 12:5, emphasis added).

Nathan pointed his long, bony finger in the king's face and said, *"Thou art the man"* (2 Sam. 12:7). David's violent temper and exaggerated response resulted from his violated conscience. He had taken Uriah's wife, had relations with her, and ordered a loyal soldier's death. Covering his sin aroused within him unholy anger.

Anxiety:

Are you overly nervous and irritable? Has the gentle dove, the Holy Spirit, taken His flight from controlling your inner soul? *"And let the peace of God rule in your hearts"* (Col. 3:15). One aspect of the fruit of the Holy

Spirit is peace. When the Holy Spirit controls us, we have peace within. Picture the role of the Spirit as a referee in your heart. When you commit a foul (sin), the referee blows his whistle. You lose your peace. The Bible promises a peace that is beyond comprehension. (See Philippians 4:7.) Anxiety and nervousness may be due to several reasons, one of which is an unclear conscience. It's the divine referee calling attention to a foul.

Critical Mindset:

God has not called us to act as a spiritual Gestapo. It is not our place to preside as judge over mankind. Of course, we are called to judge righteous judgment, but that kind of judging is very different from having a judgmental, hypercritical attitude. Criticism is often a defense mechanism people use to justify themselves. When distrust, suspicion, and cynicism become an obsession, they are sure signs of a deeper problem. If you are proficient at faultfinding and making analytical indictments, carefully consider this verse: *"Therefore thou art inexcusable, O man, whosoever thou art that judgest: for wherein thou judgest another, thou condemnest thyself; for thou that judgest doest the same things"* (Rom. 2:1).

Have you noticed that the things that bother you about other people are generally the same things of which you yourself are guilty? It's so much easier to condemn someone else than to admit that you're in the same boat! I believe one of the Puritans said, "Where the devil doesn't go personally, he sends a critic." The accuser of the brethren dispatches his "assistants" to speak for him. When you're critical, you can't love your friends, much less your enemies. Such is the bitter fruit of a violated conscience.

Lack of Love:

Are you able to articulate a detailed catalog of hurts? Is this list contrary to the characteristics of love found in First Corinthians 13? Charity (love) is kind, envies not, is not puffed up, is not easily provoked, thinks no evil, bears all things, rejoices not in evil, hopes all things, and endures all things. What a description of love! Do you have an attitude problem? Do you lack love?

God is love. Love, the chief fruit of the Spirit, is the greatest motivator in the world. When *"...the love of God is shed abroad in our hearts..."* (Rom. 5:5), we are granted the supernatural ability to empathize and show concern. An absence of love is proof that we have grieved the Spirit.

We are called to be like Jesus: broken bread and poured-out wine. Our position is that of servants, love slaves of Jesus Christ. When compassion is missing, it is likely due to a disturbed conscience.

Guilt:

Do you struggle with feeling guilty about events in your past? Does this guilt occupy your mind and make you unable to concentrate? Are you forever preaching to yourself, *"If only I had never..."* or *"I wish I had..."*? Are you tormented by plaguing thoughts of regret?

Guilt is God's means to bring us to a place of repentance, humility, and brokenness. As we have seen, the blood of Jesus cleanses the guilty sinner. With Calvary and the brokenness of Jesus in view, we are compelled to appeal there for mercy from the Lord and are enabled to make amends with our fellow man. Once we see the Creator's brokenness for our sin, it is only right that we are broken over our sin. Brokenness is a necessary prerequisite for restitution. Never rationalize the things over which you need to repent. It is not God's will for you to live depressed, defeated, and dejected. He wants *"our hearts sprinkled from an evil conscience"* (Heb. 10:22).

Joylessness:

Do you often feel despondent and fatigued? Has your zest for life waned? Have you lost the joy of His salvation? When your cup of joy isn't overflowing, you may have a leak in it. Nothing drains energy and depletes joy faster than a soiled conscience.

Like love and peace, joy is also a fruit of the Spirit. Inner joy, with cups running over, is a tremendous benefit of life in Christ. The pathway to freedom is cleansing, forgiveness, and restoration.

Self-Condemnation:

Belittling yourself is neither healthy nor helpful. When the conscience is guilty, how easy it is to take a stick to ourselves. Self-induced floggings, whether verbal or merely mental, only complicate the dilemma. Some mistake self-criticism for humility. In reality, it is the exact opposite; it is pride. Pride doesn't always manifest itself as haughtiness; sometimes it disguises itself as mock humility. Self-condemnation is the opposite of true brokenness. God wants obedience, not self-degradation. Evading responsibility is just another tactic to bypass responsibility to God and man.

Abnormal Fears:

One man told me he had such a fear of heights that he was afraid to go to a building's second floor. That inordinate fear is totally unnatural. Fear is sometimes a byproduct of a guilty conscience. God has not given us a spirit of fear, but of love, power, and a disciplined mind. (See 2 Timothy 1:7.) How many fears are complications from inner guilt? Perfect love casts out fear. (See 1 John 4:18.) Love is demonstrated through obedience. Jesus said, *"If ye love me, keep my commandments"* (John 14:15). Often, irrational fears vanish when the conscience is cleared by obedience.

Externals and Activity:

In order to pacify a guilty conscience, some over-emphasize external conformity and religious activity. To compensate for guilt from the past, they set a high standard, be it external conformity or secret pride in abstaining from certain practices. Jesus spoke of the Pharisees, who were outwardly clean but inwardly defiled. (See Luke 11:39.) Strict adherence to self-imposed codes and constant activity while neglecting real priorities are poor substitutes for genuine restoration.

Isolation:

The man concealing a violated conscience cannot afford to allow others to get *too close*. He always faces the danger of being found out. Keeping a small circle of friends at a distance minimizes the possibilities of exposure. Without brokenness, he cannot experience openness; and without openness, he cannot experience oneness. So he withdraws and isolates himself.

Defensiveness:

Only the teachable can be taught and only the approachable can be approached. The book of Proverbs describes the wise man who benefits from corrective rebukes while fools despise instruction. (See Proverbs 9:7-9.) It is possible to rationalize and justify just about anything. *"All the ways of a man are clean in his own eyes; but the Lord weigheth the spirits"* (Prov. 16:2). Defensive barriers, rather than protecting, obstruct the true healing that comes only through reconciliation.

REFLECTIONS

1. The purpose of God's commands is to produce purity, a sincere faith, and a good conscience. (See 1 Timothy 1:5.)

2. David's explosive and exaggerated responses were due to unresolved guilt. Clearing the conscience restores balance in our souls.

3. Self-condemnation is neither healthy nor helpful.

4. Defensive barriers, rather than protecting, obstruct the true healing that comes only through reconciliation.

STUDY QUESTIONS AND POINTS OF APPLICATION

1. Skim through the list of indicators of a defiled conscience as described in this

chapter. Which one(s) apply to you? Make a note of them.

2. Ask the Lord to search your heart and reveal offenses you have committed that have produced these symptoms. List the names of those you have offended. After completing item three below, take appropriate steps to clear your conscience.

3. As a Bible study, go through the Beatitudes (Matt. 5:3-12) and relate each of the eleven indicators of a violated conscience to one or more of the attitudes reflected in the Beatitudes. Clearing the conscience requires not only going but also going with the right spirit or attitude. Which godly attitudes do you need to cultivate in your life as you prepare to clear your conscience?

CHAPTER 11

HOW DO I CLEAR MY CONSCIENCE?

We can avoid many adverse results by living in obedience to God's Word. In the realm of a clear conscience, we have only two ways to be happy in Jesus. They are to trust and obey.

The conscience is an inward monitor that gauges our inclinations and actions. The purpose of the conscience is to correct and reprimand us when we do wrong or are about to do wrong. It is a delicate instrument that, when working correctly, is sensitively tuned. Yet it is not oversensitive. The conscience functions as an inner alarm that forewarns us of potential danger. There is no alternative to a clear conscience. Hard work, excellent knowledge, or strong emotions are no substitute for a conscience that is fine-tuned by the Holy Spirit and the Holy Word.

Some have described the conscience as the window of the soul. Dirt, dust, and smut will hinder light from passing through a window. A sufficient coat of filth will totally block out the light. The conscience is a window through which God's light shines to expose our faults. When we submit to His voice and eliminate the sin He condemns, God reinforces the strength and clarity of our conscience. The light shines brighter next time. But when we don't obediently respond to the inner voice, our conscience becomes hardened or desensitized, and sin accumulates. When this occurs, the window is clouded, and light barely penetrates. The conscience can become seared or paralyzed. (See 1 Timothy 4:2.) In this state, we have no grief for sin and only a dull sensitivity to the voice of God. This condition spells serious trouble!

Christianity is a religion of the conscience. It is more than adherence to externals; it is about a heart in tune with God. Once we are convicted that a wrong needs to be put right, we must either obey or violate our conscience. Titus 1:15 refers to a defiled conscience. When the conscience is defiled, it acts like a faulty thermostat; it doesn't respond properly at the right time. It is out of step with where we should be. The Bible speaks of a "good conscience" (1 Tim. 1:5; 1 Pet. 3:16). Paul said, *"And herein do I exercise myself, to have always a conscience void of offence toward God, and toward men"* (Acts 24:16). But how do we recalibrate our conscience so it is *"void of offence"*?

The clearing of the conscience is twofold: toward God and toward man. Old Testament sacrifices and ceremonies were insufficient to cleanse the conscience. (See Hebrews 9:9; 10:1-2.) So, in the course of time, God sent His Son. *"For if the blood of bulls and of goats, and the ashes of an heifer sprinkling the unclean, sanctifieth to the purifying of the flesh: How much more shall the blood of Christ, who through the eternal Spirit offered himself without spot to God, **purge your conscience** from dead works to serve the living God?"* (Heb. 9:13-14, emphasis added).

In Kenya, Africa, when someone in the Maasai tribe wants to resolve an offense, he takes a goat to the offended party. Then he slits the goat's throat and gives the dying goat to the offended party. Those immersed in this culture have a saying, "Where the blood flows, forgiveness comes." And blood flowed on Calvary so forgiveness could come to sinful men.

So powerful is the blood of Jesus that it puts us in good standing in God's sight and bids us come boldly into the holiest. (See Hebrews 10:19.) On the cross, Jesus dealt with our guilt, our sins, and everything in us that defies God. The forgiveness of sins is not only judicial but also experiential. In other words, the cleansing by Christ's blood is so deep that the forgiven sinner should feel it. No wonder we are challenged to *"draw near...in full assurance of faith, having our hearts sprinkled from an evil conscience"* (Heb. 10:22). How does this forgiveness happen on a practical level?

It begins with a confession: *"But if we walk in the light, as he is in the light, we have fellowship one with another, and the blood of Jesus Christ his Son cleanseth us from all sin"* (1 John 1:7).

Walking in the light is simply a willingness to get out in the open. When the light exposes the darkness in our lives, we should immediately confess and forsake it. We should not hide, deny, or rationalize. We must agree with God about our sins. Simply put, the way to walk in the light is to keep the conscience clean by responding immediately and completely to it. Forgiveness comes through confession. Cleansing comes through walking in the light because, as we walk in the light, the blood of Jesus cleanses us. And when we walk in the light, we never walk alone. The Scripture says that *"we have fellowship one with another"* (1 John 1:7). We have fellowship with God and everyone else who is walking in the light.

The blood of Christ makes the conscience faultless before God. If our conscience is to be clear toward man, it is so because we have acted to put things right. After his conversion, Zacchaeus paid back everyone whom he had cheated. (See Luke 19:8.) Remember Jesus' words: *"first be reconciled"* (Matt. 5:24). Having a good conscience is invaluable. The goal of Bible instruction is to bring about a clear conscience. That means I must settle my I-owe-you list.

In Bible times, the towns and villages likely had a silversmith in residence. This silversmith had a shop and a large pot for melting metal. The smith placed the metal ore in the pot over a fire hot enough to melt the ore. Once the aggregate was liquefied, impurities floated to the top, and the smith skimmed off the scum. The metal cooled and hardened. Then the smith built a hotter fire under the pot, and hotter temperatures caused a different type of impurity to surface. This process was repeated with more intense heat each time and, with each, it brought different types of impurities to the surface. In each case, the smith skimmed off the filth.

The heat brought about by the friction of human relationships causes our impurities to surface. People do not create pollutions within us, but they can cause them to surface. Someone once said, "If you want to know what you are full of, see what spills out when you're jostled." No one can make you hate; nevertheless, relationships can bring out hidden problems. The heat doesn't cause the scum; it merely exposes what's inside. Suppose the metal ore was liquefied and an awful froth surfaced. Unless the smith ladled it off, it would sink back into the metal as it cooled. It wouldn't even be visible until the heat was reapplied, and then it would reappear. When contaminations surface, we must deal with them. Nobody likes dealing with scum, but that step is absolutely necessary.

When relationships heat up—in the home, church, or business—and impurities surface, we have several choices. First, we can run from the fire. But running brings only temporary relief. When problems heat up a marriage, many abandon their commitment and marry someone else. Initially, angry emotions subside as things cool down. But it won't take long before more friction brings forth heat and the residual problems resurface. Running from the problem and getting out of the fire will never solve anything. That choice merely allows our inner impurities to submerge and settle where they're undetected, but the contaminants are still there. God's way is not to avoid all conflicts but to learn the proper response in each situation.

Second, we can deal with the defilement. Changing churches each time something goes wrong is not the answer. Examples from Scripture indicate that God is more concerned about our response than about what actually happens to us. Offenses will occur. People will offend us, and their offenses can reveal ugly attitudes and trigger wrong responses. Thorough cleansing calls for thorough dealing with the scum each time it surfaces. The job is messy. But it's the only way to be cleansed.

The pressure of dealing with others is God's way of purifying His people. The Spirit labors to knock out, knock off, and lift off everything in us that is unlike Jesus. Purification is a process. The silversmith heats and skims, then heats the ore hotter and skims again. He does this over and over until the liquid silver is so pure that he can look at it and see the reflection of his face. This purifying is what God is doing with us. He wants us to be so holy that He can see His own image in us. Oh, the blessing of a clear conscience!

REFLECTIONS

1. The conscience is an inward monitor that gauges our inclinations and actions. It also forewarns us of impending danger.

2. When we don't obediently respond to the inner voice, our conscience becomes hardened or desensitized and sin accumulates.

3. Relational conflict causes impurities to surface.

4.   A clear conscience has a vertical and a horizontal dimension: *"...void of offence toward God, and toward man"* (Acts 24:16).

STUDY QUESTIONS AND POINTS OF APPLICATION

1.   What is the purpose of the conscience?

2.   Describe God's major purpose in our lives through relationships with others and the hurts they bring.

3.   The Christian goes into spiritual warfare with only two major weapons: faith and a good conscience (1 Tim. 1:19). How do we gain and maintain such a conscience?

4.   Forgiveness comes through confession. Cleansing comes by walking in the light. Describe the difference between forgiveness and cleansing.

CHAPTER 12

HOW DO I ASK FOR FORGIVENESS?

Now comes the all-important matter of acting on what you know you must do. Don't rush recklessly into forgiveness without first mapping out a scriptural path. The Bible gives clear directions for seeking forgiveness. God must prepare the way. In many situations, there is no question about immediate action. In other cases, the Lord must initiate it. Be willing to obey God as He opens the door. Pray right now, "Lord, I am willing to make restitution just as soon as the way is prepared." When the Lord opens the door, act immediately. In some instances, it is important that the other party first be ready to receive you. God will make the timing clear as you are in tune with Him. Sometimes the reception may not be positive. But when you move in God's timing, He will move in the way He planned and bring about His desired results.

When granting forgiveness, you must tear up your You-Owe-Me list. But when seeking forgiveness, you must make your own I-Owe-You list. List the people you have hurt and the nature of your offense. The chances are you already have such a list and your conscience forever brings it up. Ask God if other situations require attention. He will show you the instances you need to act on.

Asking for forgiveness is always one-sided. Never expect the other person to take or even share the blame. Seeking forgiveness deals only with your guilt in a given matter. As far as you are concerned, your sole responsibility is to make things right, because you are dealing only with your wrongs.

The scope of your transgression determines the scope of your confession. Confess *personal* sins to God. Deal with *private* sins only among those involved. *Public* sins call for public confession. These guidelines should always govern attempts at reconciliation.

Next, you must go to the offended party. Do you remember Jesus' instruction to leave your gift, go your way, and first be reconciled? (See Matthew 5:24.) Once

God has spoken and you know what to do, don't wait for the other person to come to you; you must go to him. Be clear in your choice of wording. Say something like this: "I am sorry. I was wrong. Will you forgive me for (name your offense)?" If the other party denies that you wronged him or tries to dismiss the matter, press him again. "God has convicted me. I was wrong. I am sorry. Will you forgive me?" Once you have obeyed God, you are free, no matter how the other party responds.

Never say, "If I offended you, I am sorry." Never stand before a congregation and say, "If I've ever hurt anyone here, please forgive me." Deal with certainties. Dealing with the *ifs* never resolves anything. If restitution deals with your blame, then it must be that you have offended or hurt others or allowed wrong attitudes to remain in your mind. Take responsibility and deal with your wrongs.

In matters of immorality, you do not need to go into detail. Rehearsing illicit episodes is an unhealthy practice. The Scriptures say that even speaking of such things is shameful. (See Ephesians 5:12.) A telephone call may be the best way to handle such cases. Writing a confession on paper is dangerous because you never know who will read it. A written confession also provides a continual reminder of your offense and may only deepen bitter feelings. Renewing acquaintances may unwisely rekindle emotions. Exercise caution. If possible, call the offended party and get right to the point. Ask for forgiveness for wrongs. A lengthy conversation is unnecessary. Say what you must to clear your conscience.

In cases of dishonesty and theft, you must make amends. You should return merchandise, pay for what you've taken, or offer a plan for repayment. After his conversion, Zacchaeus paid back four times as much as he had taken. (See Luke 19:8.) The Bible does not demand this standard, but just restitution is necessary.

Consult your pastor or spiritual leader if you are in doubt *"...in the multitude of counselors there is safety"* (Prov. 11:14). Godly counsel from mature believers may be necessary. Some cases are so delicate that you may need great wisdom. Don't hesitate to seek help from a third party.

These scriptural guidelines on granting and seeking forgiveness are essential for fruitful Christian living. Forgiveness lies at the base of our life in Christ. The Lord Jesus bore our punishment to satisfy God's justice and pardon sinners like us. Because God has forgiven us, we must forgive others who have wronged us and seek forgiveness from those we have wronged, for Christ's sake. By humbling ourselves before God and man, we can be free from guilt and experience deep inward peace. Never let pride stand in your way. Obey God no matter the cost. Obedience is better than sacrifice. (See 1 Samuel 15:22.)

REFLECTIONS

1. Asking for forgiveness is always one-sided. Never expect the other person to take or even share the blame.

2. The scope of your transgression determines the scope of your confession. Confess personal sins to God. Deal with private sins only among those involved. Public sins call for public confession.

3. Never rehearse the details of an illicit relationship. When seeking forgiveness, get to the point quickly.

4. If you are uncertain how to proceed, seek godly counsel.

STUDY QUESTIONS AND POINTS OF APPLICATION

1. After prayerfully committing yourself to obey God by seeking forgiveness, write out your I-owe-you list as mentioned in

this chapter. Top the list with the names of those you have hurt the most.

2. Which of God's commands did you violate when committing each offense? List them beside each individual's name.

3. When seeking forgiveness, what determines the scope or extent of your confession to others?

4. Go to each person from whom you need to seek forgiveness after working out a specific statement of your wrong toward him. Follow the guidelines in this chapter.

PRACTICAL STEPS WHEN SEEKING FORGIVENESS

The following summarizes what you learned in Section 2. Follow these guidelines when seeking forgiveness from those you have offended.

1. Make a list of those you have wronged. Ask God to bring to your remembrance every situation on which you need to act. Compile your personal I-owe-you list.

2. Go to God and confess your offenses as sin. Agree with Him about each situation. Thank Him for His forgiveness.

3. Tell the Lord you are willing to go to those on your list. Now you are ready to go and put things right. Some situations call for God's timing, and you may need to ask God to prepare hearts. If you are in doubt, consult with your pastor or spiritual advisor.

4. Asking for forgiveness is always one-sided as far as you are concerned. Never ask the other person to share the blame.

5. Confess personal sins to God. Acknowledge private sins to those involved. Public sins call for public confession. The scope of your transgression determines the scope of your confession. Make sure the circle of offense determines the extent of your confession.

6. Use clear wording and get to the point: "I am sorry for_____ (name your offense). I was wrong. Will you forgive me?"

7. When you need to make restitution, as in cases of stealing, make appropriate amends.

8. Don't hesitate to consult others if you are unclear about how to proceed.

9. Act in obedience! Do what you know you need to do. Confession may be difficult at first, but after you start, you will feel as if weights are being removed from your shoulders.

   Often, attempts at reconciliation are the path to restoration. But even if the other party does not respond positively, you are free after you have obeyed these scriptural principles.

10. Don't let the Enemy talk you out of obtaining God's blessing by being fully and completely obedient.

SCRUTINIZING FORGIVENESS

CHAPTER 13

ARE FORGIVENESS AND RECONCILIATION THE SAME THING?

I feel strongly that plain speaking is desperately needed when discussing the difference between forgiveness and reconciliation. All too often the entire onus is placed on the offended and his responsibility to forgive while neglecting to emphasize the offender's responsibility to repent. The offended is often persuaded into acquiescing and made to feel guilty if he is unwilling to get back to "business as usual" with an unrepentant offender. I remember an instance where a church member was caught red-handed in a matter of dishonesty. The pastor

THE POWER OF FORGIVENESS

more or less shamed the congregation into assisting the thief to pay back what he had stolen. By lessening the seriousness of the offense, this pastor did what was emotionally satisfying. But Paul wrote, *"Them that sin rebuke before all, that others also may fear"* (1 Tim. 5:20). Of course, wisdom and grace are to be employed, but spiritual authority must be brought to bear both to restore the offender and warn the church in order to prevent more problems. The blurred line between forgiveness and reconciliation definitely needs clarity. These two things are separate issues.

Seeking justice when you are wronged is entirely appropriate. But often, your offender is unwilling to make amends. And sadly, the legal system frequently works to the benefit of the perpetrator instead of the abused. In Christian circles, it's rare that church leaders follow the Bible's teaching on reconciliation. (See Matthew 18:15-17.) Seldom does a local church bring spiritual weight to bear upon the unruly. So how should you respond to those who hurt you, lie to you, rip you off, and abuse you?

The Lord Jesus shed light on this issue. Note His words:

> *Then said he unto the disciples, It is impossible but that offences will come: but woe unto him, through whom they come! It were*

better for him that a millstone were hanged about his neck, and he cast into the sea, than that he should offend one of these little ones. Take heed to yourselves: If thy brother trespass against thee, rebuke him; and if he repent, forgive him. And if he trespass against thee seven times in a day, and seven times in a day turn again to thee, saying, I repent; thou shalt forgive him (Luke 17:1-4).

In these verses, Jesus communicated:

- The seriousness of offending (tripping up, enticing to sin) God's people. Drowning with a millstone around your neck is preferable to facing a holy God over these offenses!

- When a brother sins against you, rebuke him. This means to admonish or reprimand immediately.

- If he repents (thinks differently, feels compunction, reconsiders), then forgive him. The word *forgive* means "to send away, let go, or remit." Simply put, we must let go of the offense.

- Repeated offenses call for repeated forgiveness.

- When the offender repents, the relationship is salvaged.

Some preachers teach that we should never *let go* of an offense unless the offender repents. This verse seems to indicate that interpretation. The reasoning is: since God never forgives a person unless that person repents, neither should we. Obviously, we are not God. God has plainly instructed us concerning our responsibility to forgive. Jesus gave other pertinent teaching concerning the necessity of forgiveness:

- In the model prayer we are instructed to pray, *"And forgive us our debts, as we forgive our debtors"* (Matt. 6:12).
- This is followed by: *"For if ye forgive men their trespasses, your heavenly Father will also forgive you: But if ye forgive not men their trespasses, neither will your Father forgive your trespasses"* (Matt. 6:14-15).
- These plain directives have no qualifiers attached to them. Jesus did not say, "Forgive men their trespasses when, or if, they repent." He plainly charges His followers with the responsibility to forgive.

Charles Spurgeon said, "The goal of prayer is the ear of God." If we are to access the ear of God, we must grant forgiveness.

Life is too short to carry the bitterness from yesterday's hurts. Your personal peace and well-being are not dependent upon the actions of an unrepentant person. We must choose to *do right* regardless of the reaction of our offenders. Ephesians 4:32 also states, *"And be ye kind one to another, tenderhearted, forgiving one another, even as God for Christ's sake hath forgiven you."* Again, here is a straightforward imperative: *"forgiving one another"* just like Christ has forgiven you. If repentance were a prerequisite for human forgiveness, then you and I would have to carry a lot of baggage in our hearts until the day we die. These wounds must be laid to rest, and forgiveness (letting go) is God's prescription in such cases.

To reiterate, *forgive* means "to release a debt." This is a judicial act between you and God. You should pray it out:

> *Lord, I've been hurt and angry, but I choose to forgive (name of the offender). It's out of my hands. I will no longer seek vengeance. It's now between You and that person. I release the debt I've been holding against him/her. I choose to forgive (name of the offender). Thank you for forgiving me and restoring peace in my spirit. Amen.*

Forgiveness is a private matter. It takes only two to forgive: you and God. But reconciliation requires three:

you, God, and your offender. Restoration calls for humility and repentance on the part of your offender.

Once you are clear in your spirit on the matter of forgiveness, then you must decide how you will relate to your offender. Reestablishing fellowship is impossible apart from that person owning his or her actions and putting things right. Forgiveness is not pretending that no offense was committed. You are under no obligation to maintain a close relationship or conduct business with an untrustworthy individual or business entity. The only way to deal with *shady characters* is to walk away from them. (I'm speaking here about voluntary relationships.) People who are dishonest cannot be trusted. Dishonest people who attend church are still dishonest. Religious crooks are still crooks. And until they repent, you are *not* duty-bound to maintain a working relationship with them. Have you forgiven? Yes! Do you need to open yourself to more abuse? *No!*

After you have done all in your power to reconcile, you are free to walk away with a clear conscience. It is counterproductive to tell an unrepentant person that he is forgiven. Such a person doesn't think he needs to be forgiven! You should never feel compelled to explain your choice to forgive to anyone who is not seeking forgiveness. So, after you have attempted to *make things right,* you should deal *only* with God about your hurt and bitterness. Remember that forgiveness is a decision, not an emotion. It is a choice and not a feeling. Never live in bondage to your emotions. You must *do* right because it *is* right, regardless of how you feel. Once you choose to do the right thing, your emotions will stablize in time.

It's your responsibility to forgive. But it's your offender's responsibility to repent and participate in reconciliation. As much as possible, live peaceably with all men. (See Romans 12:18.) Don't let an oversensitive conscience drag you back to individuals you need to avoid.

REFLECTIONS

1. Jesus instructed us to rebuke a brother if he sins against us. This means to admonish or reprimand immediately.

2. The word *forgive* means "to send away, let go, or remit." Simply put, we must let go of the offense.

3. Forgiveness is a private matter. It takes only two to forgive: you and God. But reconciliation requires three: you, God, and your offender.

4. You are under no obligation to maintain a close relationship or conduct business

with an untrustworthy individual or business entity.

STUDY QUESTIONS AND POINTS OF APPLICATION

1. What is the difference between forgiveness and reconciliation?

2. Forgiveness is a choice to let go of an offense. Is it wise to inform an unrepentant person you have forgiven him or her?

3. Forgiveness takes place in an instant. But inner healing and emotional stabilizing take time. Aren't you glad that forgiveness is not an emotion?

4. How should we respond to shady characters who have wronged us?

CHAPTER 14

WHAT ABOUT BRAWLERS?

Some people are not content unless they are agitating or attacking someone. They thrive on conflict. They seem restless unless they are in a battle. If no conflict is brewing, they will start one. Someone noted, "People who have no life of their own want to start drama in yours."

The Bible refers to these quarrelsome types as "brawlers" (Titus 3:2). Their arrogance puffs them up, and in turn, they set themselves up as judges. Brawlers are contentious, cantankerous, and argumentative. They sow division and feed on discord. These wranglers birth contention in every environment. They are lightning rods for controversy and obsessed with negativity. The Bible speaks about how to deal with belligerent and combative individuals.

Brawlers, or quarrelers, are disqualified from spiritual leadership. *"A man that is an heretick* [schismatic, divisive] *after the first and second admonition* [mild rebuke] *reject* [shun]*; Knowing that he that is such is subverted* [perverted]*, and sinneth, being condemned of himself"* (Titus 3:10-11).

Rather than owning his sin and cleansing his guilty conscience, the schismatic goes on the attack, sowing strife and discord. It has been accurately stated, "Hurt people hurt other people. Troubled people cause trouble." Their diseased souls spread misery and friction. And until they find inner healing, they cause turmoil wherever they go. Some ministries and churches were built on controversy, and were ruined by the same. Beware of the pulpits that repeatedly speak negatively of *other churches* in favor of their own. Persistent criticism is often evidence of a guilty conscience. Once a divisive person has been reproved twice, steer clear of that person. When it comes to a quarreler, the wisest thing you can do is stay away from him or her.

You have a scriptural mandate to disassociate yourself and your family from the spiritual abuse of a contentious person. Your emotional well-being and peace of mind demand withdrawal from these peace-stealers. If you study the epistles, you may be shocked at the number of admonitions to walk away from divisive people. Here are some Scriptures that call for separation from conflict-ridden individuals:

*Now I beseech you, brethren, mark them which cause divisions and offences contrary to the doctrine which ye have learned; and **avoid them*** (Romans 16:17, emphasis added).

*Now we command you, brethren, in the name of our Lord Jesus Christ, that ye **withdraw yourselves** from every brother that walketh disorderly, and not after the tradition which he received of us* (2 Thessalonians 3:6, emphasis added).

*And if any man obey not our word by this epistle, note that man, and **have no company** with him, that he may be ashamed* (2 Thessalonians 3:14, emphasis added).

*Having a form of godliness, but denying the power thereof: **from such turn away*** (2 Timothy 3:5, emphasis added).

Dishonest behavior and lying are seldom isolated events. Any person who lies without repenting will lie again. The man who gossips to you will gossip about you. Mark it down, any man who is dishonest with you will speak dishonestly about you. His lack of integrity toward God and man is evidence of a seared conscience. Paul remarked that in the latter days some will depart from the faith by giving heed to doctrines of demons. He went on to describe those who fall away: "...*speaking lies in hypocrisy; having their conscience seared with a hot iron*" (1 Tim. 4:1-2). A hardened conscience is desensitized and easily justifies wrong behavior. Without a functioning conscience, an individual grows to follow his twisted ways habitually. This path of digression leads to spiritual oblivion. He becomes worse and worse. And the worse he becomes, the less he knows it! You cannot help people with a seared conscience, but they can harm you.

Avoid those who unsettle your peace of mind like a plague. Just because some people are addicted to drama does not mean you have to attend their performances. You are not obligated to entertain anyone who poisons your sense of well-being. Life is too precious to give a self-absorbed narcissist permission to bully, badger, belittle, or bug you. Notice some characteristics of contaminated individuals. They are toxic people. They...

- Thrive on contention,
- Constantly criticize,
- Exude negativity,
- Resist correction,
- Are self-absorbed,
- Slander with ease,

- Impugn motives,
- Emanate arrogance,
- Attack without remorse,
- Alienate others.

To simplify, toxic relationships do not assist you in loving God or people. They keep you distracted and hinder you from carrying out your assignment. Walking away from contaminated, voluntary relationships will improve your life immensely. The only way to get along with some people is by moving on without them! Put the drama behind you, and the path in front of you will grow brighter.

REFLECTIONS

1. People who have no life of their own want to start drama in yours.

2. You have a scriptural mandate to disassociate yourself and your family from the spiritual abuse of a contentious person.

3. Dishonest behavior and lying are seldom isolated events. The man who gossips to you will gossip about you.

4. You are not obligated to entertain anyone who poisons your sense of well-being.

STUDY QUESTIONS AND POINTS OF APPLICATION

1. What does Titus 3:10-11 teach about relating to divisive individuals?

2. Review the Scriptures listed that demand separation from conflict-ridden people.

3. What are the characteristics of a "toxic" person?

4. Be watchful and observe abusive patterns that continue after two admonitions.

CHAPTER 15

HOW TO GET BEYOND YOUR HURTS

Rehearsing your hurts cultivates bitterness. Rehearsing negative experiences cultivates a critical spirit. Obsessing over negativity breeds cynicism. But rehearsing your blessings will cultivate a grateful heart.

The importance of your meditations and conversations cannot be overstated. Your mind and your mouth affect you and those around you in profound ways. Your thoughts, or meditations, define you. As a man *"thinketh in his heart, so is he"* (Prov. 23:7). Every man is responsible for the thoughts he thinks. You can choose to dwell on things that are pure, honest, just, and the like. (See Philippians 4:8.) Or you can choose to meditate on destructive things. Our minds are always dwelling on something, and we must break wrong thought patterns by acquiring new ones.

To clear your mind of harmful thoughts, you must begin by eliminating negative words from your mouth. Like a rudder on a ship and a bridle on a horse, your words give direction to your life. (See James 3:3-5.) Both *"death and life are in the power of the tongue."* (See Proverbs 18:21.) Your speech may give birth, or it may kill. This is why you must be deliberate in how you utilize words. Start speaking words of life instead of words of death. Your speech is programing you and everyone around you. To remove wrong thoughts from your mind, begin by eliminating wrong words from your mouth.

Prayer is talking with God. Meditation is talking to yourself. A conversation is talking with others. Your tongue is a little member, but it has huge consequences in all three realms: prayer, meditation, and conversation. Words can kill dreams, friendships, and even faith. Notice the warning from James about the tongue: *"And the tongue is a fire and a world of iniquity…it defileth the whole body,…and it is set on fire of hell."* (See James 3:6.)

Someone said, "The tongue is so hot that God had to place it in a wet solution, else it would burn our heads off!" Flaming tongues can do a world of damage.

Pay close attention to how you talk with yourself and others.

Yes, there is a battle for your mind. The war on the saints takes place largely between the ears. But you have powerful weapons with which to rein in those renegade thoughts. (See 2 Corinthians 10:3-5.) This mental warfare can be intense, but you can demolish strongholds. You are not a victim of fate. Your thoughts are not predetermined. When you feel out of control and your mind is racing, you must learn to employ the powerful weapons at your disposal. Thinking right thoughts and speaking right words will set the course for your life.

Stop grumbling and start thanking. Instead of brooding on your hurts, begin to give thanks for your blessings. Stop dwelling on what you have lost and be grateful for what you have left. Since your mouth and your mind are intrinsically connected, each influences the other. Our innermost thoughts and even our whispers are consequential. Choosing "good thoughts" and speaking "right words" are mandatory.

David prayed, *"Let the words of my mouth, and the meditation of my heart, be acceptable in thy sight, O Lord, my strength, and my redeemer"* (Ps. 19:14). This was a preventative prayer. He was thinking about what lay ahead and appealed to God for help and strength. He wanted his speech and thinking to be appropriate and proper. So he cried out to the Lord for His empowerment. He wanted his conversations and meditations to be acceptable to God.

The good news is our minds can be reprogrammed. Thanking God in advance is the first step of faith. There comes a point in prayer where we need to move from requesting to believing. It's the difference between asking and appropriating God's resources. When a person thanks God for something before it becomes apparent, that is faith. *"Now faith is the substance of things hoped for, the evidence of things not seen"* (Heb. 11:1). Notice that faith is substantive. It is the title deed for a request, the evidence of things we do not currently see. Prayer is the means to bring the future into the present. It is God's ordained way to import God's will from heaven to earth. They are not prayers of doubt but prayers of faith that move God's hand. Faith-filled praying expects an answer and dares to thank God ahead of time! Faith honors God and God honors faith.

The hurts and wounds you have suffered do not deserve continued mental airtime. Dwelling on these things generates anger and resentment. Don't let those injuries define you. You must stop walking down those painful corridors in your mind. You can chart a new course for a brighter tomorrow by leaving those dark places behind. The key element in transitioning from a victim of circumstance to a life of overcoming is by guarding your mind and your mouth.

A young woman was attending a Bible college where she was raped. As a result, she found herself pregnant. She chose to place her baby in an adopted home. She was healed of that horrific experience. Out of her misery came her ministry. Today, she runs an adoption agency where she assists mothers in placing their babies in loving Christian homes. Bad experiences are not the final chapter unless you permit them to be. You have the power to move beyond your pain.

You can cultivate a grateful spirit by rehearsing your blessings. You can cultivate an expectant spirit by learning to thank God in advance. Faith is the only way to please God. *"Giving thanks always for all things unto God and the Father in the name of our Lord Jesus Christ"* (Eph. 5:20). Repetitive complaining will attract more things to complain about. Repeated gratitude will attract more things for which to be thankful. Repetitive gratitude builds your confidence in God. Thanking God ahead of time will move you from a mentality of defeat to a stance of faith. A faith-filled, forward focus is of great assistance in getting beyond your past hurts.

REFLECTIONS

1. Rehearsing your hurts will cultivate bitterness. Rehearsing your blessings will cultivate a grateful heart.

2. To clear your mind of destructive thoughts, you must begin by eliminating negative words from your mouth.

3. The key element in transitioning from a victim of circumstance to a life of overcoming is by bridling your mind and your mouth.

4. Prayer is talking with God. Meditation is talking to yourself. A conversation is talking with others. There is power in your mouth!

STUDY QUESTIONS AND POINTS OF APPLICATION

1. Look up and read Proverbs 23:7 now. What does this verse teach?

2. What is the correlation between conversation and meditation?

3. The battle for your mind takes place between your ears. Review Second

Corinthians 10:3-5 and list the advantages we have because of our spiritual weapons.

4. Instead of continually complaining, start practicing repeated gratitude. Rehearse your blessings before the Lord now.

CHAPTER 16

Cut or Untangle?

There's a time to walk away from harmful relationships. There are also many times when you just need some space. When someone unleashes on you, you may need to back away from that person for a season. Never allow an isolated incident or difference of opinion to be the cause of severing a meaningful relationship. Sooner or later we all say things, do things, and think things that are damaging. Someone once said, "When a friend makes a mistake, don't rub it in; rub it out!"

Paul encourages us to put up with one another: *"With all lowliness and meekness, with longsuffering, forbearing one another in love; Endeavoring to keep the unity of the Spirit in the bond of peace"* (Eph. 4:2-3). The word *forbear* means "to put up with, endure, or tolerate." So don't rend what you can repair. Don't amputate what you can arbitrate. Don't sever what can be salvaged. Don't cut what you can untangle. Do all you can to resolve relational breakdowns because it's better to *resolve* a relationship than *dissolve* a relationship. Note Paul's exhortation, *"Endeavoring to keep the unity..."* (Eph. 4:2-3). The word *endeavor* means "to be prompt and earnest in attempts to restore oneness." Maintaining personal relationships requires diligence. It is worth the effort.

All who are forgiven by God have the capacity to extend the grace they received to those who offend them. Mature people know that a temporary recess is better than retaliation. Time does not heal all wounds, but it does take time for wounds to heal. Distance influences our perspective. Nothing is as bad as it seems at first. What seems *huge* today will not be as big of a deal later. We must learn to resize our experiences. We do that by refusing to rehearse our hurts. Instead of replaying hurtful memories or verbalizing our pain, we must learn to limit our thoughts. And we can minimize our hurts by magnifying our benefits.

William James commented, "The greatest discovery of my generation is that a person can alter his life by altering his attitude of mind." This means our minds can be bent in a beneficial direction instead of a harmful one. The scenes we see on the screen of our mind can be

altered by deliberately choosing our thoughts. Paul outlined the categories for our meditations in Philippians
4:8: *"True…honest…just…pure…lovely* [acceptable]…
good report [reputable]…*virtue* [excellent]…*praise* [com-
mendable].*"* Sticking with these eight qualifiers will
eliminate the majority of the things we think about
throughout the day! We must constantly monitor our
thoughts. Any contemplations that are outside of the
categories mentioned here in Philippians must be elim-
inated. If we first untangle our thoughts, we will then
find it easier to untangle relational issues.

And the easiest way to eradicate unhealthy thoughts
is by obsessing on positive ones. For example, instead of
mentally reviewing your past mistakes, start practicing
intentional gratitude. Write down the things in your
life that are true, honest, just, pure, reputable, excellent,
and praiseworthy. After you document things worthy
of your consideration, thank God specifically for every
gift and every blessing.

It's okay to tell God how confused, hurt, and bothered you are. But instead of rehashing your dilemma
time after time, begin the habit of praying more like
this: "Lord, I thank You for Your guidance, wisdom,
power, grace, peace, strength, restoration, healing, etc."
It may be necessary to ignore your lack of emotion and
express thanks anyway. You can thank God whether
you *feel* thankful or not. Intentional gratitude moves

beyond the whims and waves of changing passions. Preoccupation with good things instead of fixating on unpleasant things is an art you can learn.

Begin to pray prayers of faith: "Lord, I trust You for_____." And "Lord, I thank You that You will _____." Or "Lord, I believe You to_____." Practice these faith-based prayers daily for four to six weeks and you will reprogram your mind.

Moving on is essential to get free from the penitentiary of offense. You don't have to stay incarcerated. You have the power and resources to get back on the path of life. Your thoughts are your choice. When you are consumed with your blessings, your burdens will lessen. What you think determines what you do. What you do influences how you feel. And how you feel is the result of your focus. Let go of the stuff that keeps you bound.

Offenses are unavoidable. Misunderstandings are inevitable. But the scriptural mandates of forgiveness and forbearance are the blueprint for disentangling conflicts. Never undo what you can unravel. Don't cut what you can untie.

REFLECTIONS

1. Never allow an isolated incident or difference of opinion to be the cause of

severing a meaningful relationship. Don't cut what you can untangle.

2. Forgiveness is releasing a debt. As you release your debts, your spirit is liberated.

3. When you get consumed with your blessings, your burdens will lessen.

4. Endeavor to repair relational breakdowns because it's better to resolve a relationship than dissolve a relationship.

STUDY QUESTIONS AND POINTS OF APPLICATION

1. What does "forbearing" or "bearing with one another" mean in Ephesians 4:2-3?

2. List the eight adjectives cataloged in Philippians 4:8.

3. Write down the things in your life that correspond to these categories. Do this daily for a predetermined length of time.

4. Think and try to discern if you have associations that need untangling.

CHAPTER 17

WHAT IS JESUS' STRATEGY FOR RESTORATION?

Many of us, especially those with overly sensitive consciences, struggle when relational conflicts remain unresolved. We want so badly for things to *work out*. Often, however, the relationships remain strained. The difficulty is only intensified when dealing with professing Christians. Scripture is not silent on the subject of relational conflict. Jesus was meticulous in giving a strategy to reconcile when offenses occur. Carefully notice Jesus' instructions found in Matthew 18:15: *"Moreover if thy brother shall trespass against thee, go and tell him his fault between thee and him alone: if he shall hear thee, thou hast gained thy brother."*

Step One

When a fellow believer causes offense, the teaching of Scripture is to approach that person *alone* concerning his trespass. Since the scope of the offense involves only you and your offender, the initial approach must be limited to this small circle. Jesus said, *"...go and tell him his fault."* Confrontation is difficult but necessary. You must take the initiative to make the first move toward reconciliation by dealing face to face with your offender. When a definitive offense occurs, you must go alone and deal with it.

Step Two

*"But if he will not hear thee, **then** take with thee one or two more, that in the mouth of two or three witnesses every word may be established"* (Matt. 18:16, emphasis added). Should step one prove unsuccessful, Jesus said to take one or two witnesses for the sake of verification and clarification. Church leaders, or spiritually mature people, are now part of the plan to restore the broken relationship. The witness/witnesses are a vital part of this process. This is how the body of Christ functions together in restoring a relationship.

Step Three

"And if he shall neglect to hear them, tell it unto the church" (Matt. 18:17). If the offending party remains defiant,

then it becomes a public matter within the church body. Involving the assembly is meant to bring positive pressure to bear upon *sinning brothers and sisters.* I realize this sounds extreme to many who have been brought up with sentimentalized spirituality. The goal of this strategy is to bring about repentance and restoration instead of giving a pass for overt sin. Real love cares enough to confront.

Superficial religion lets things slide. Scores of churches sweep things under the carpet rather than *care-fronting* offenders. And most churches have so much *under the carpet* that it makes it difficult for anyone to walk *in the Spirit!* Love does not overlook obvious wrongs. A strong love for God and others is evident when we *care* enough to confront these problems. I believe one of the main reasons for the powerlessness of congregations is linked to corporate disobedience in matters of church discipline. It is powerfully discouraging when spiritual authorities choose to neglect God's disciplinary mandates.

STEP FOUR

"But if he neglect to hear the church, let him be unto thee as an heathen man and a publican" (Matt. 18:17). Let me be clear, the goal of church discipline is restoration. Should these steps fail to bring about repentance and reinstatement, then the offender is to be regarded as an

unsaved individual. He becomes an evangelistic prospect instead of a member in good standing.

Jesus followed up these steps with clear teaching on the role of the church's authority on earth. He said, *"Whatsoever ye shall bind on earth shall be bound in heaven: and whatsoever ye shall loose on earth shall be loosed in heaven. Again I say unto you, That if two of you shall agree on earth as touching any thing that they shall ask, it shall be done for them of my Father which is in heaven. For where two or three are gathered together in my name, there am I in the midst of them"* (Matt. 18:18-20). Think about the scope of *binding* and *loosing* referenced here. God has delegated authority to His church. He calls on congregations to share in the process of restoring erring members. There is tremendous power in agreement.

One of the most misquoted Scriptures concerning prayer is claiming that *two or three* persons gathered in Jesus' name will secure His presence in prayer. This verse is not referring to prayer in general. Instead, Christ promises His presence when His church cares enough about God's reputation to bring spiritual authority to bear on believers who are caught up in sin. Christ promises His personal presence in this uncomfortable, but necessary, matter of housecleaning. The zeal for God's name and God's glory is entirely absent when spiritual leaders refuse to follow God's mandate to deal with sin within their camp. I heard someone say, "When church discipline goes out the window, Christ walks out the door."

Disobedience is the first step toward apostasy. Failure to condemn sin is condoning sin. When a ministry tolerates evil, it is teaching observers that compromise of truth is acceptable. Whatever you permit, you promote. Silence is sanctioned. Whatever a congregation tolerates, it teaches.

Paul addressed the issue of moral sin in the Corinthian church. Fornication was common among that church body. But even worse was their toleration of a man who had taken up with his father's wife. The leadership overlooked this grievous evil. The apostle rebuked them sharply and admonished them to deal severely with this matter by putting the man out of the fellowship. Notice how serious Paul was about purity in the Corinthian church: *"In the name of our Lord Jesus Christ, when ye are gathered together, and my spirit, with the power of our Lord Jesus Christ, To deliver such an one* [the man involved in immorality] *unto Satan for the destruction of the flesh, that the spirit may be saved in the day of the Lord Jesus"* (1 Cor. 5:4-5). A holy God calls His followers to holy living. Many American churches may have repudiated holiness, but God has not changed His standards. (See 1 Corinthians 5:1-8.)

Paul goes on:

> *I wrote unto you in an epistle not to company with fornicators.... But now I have written unto you not to keep company, if any man that is called a brother be a fornicator, or covetous, or an idolater, or a railer, or a drunkard, or an extortioner; with such an one no not to eat. For what have I to do to judge them also that are without? do not ye judge them that are within?...Therefore put away from among yourselves that wicked person* (1 Corinthians 5:9, 11-13).

This is how biblical Christianity functions. This approach may seem harsh to those caught up in contemporary, cultural religiosity. But God's holiness demands purity within His church. Integrity is not optional. Personal and practical holiness call for separation from evil. Corporate holiness requires the confrontation of compromise and sinful behavior. Paul did not mince words: *"Them that sin rebuke before all, that others also may fear"* (1 Tim. 5:20). Spiritual oversight is a deterrent to sin as well as a reminder that God's church is serious about holiness. When the steps outlined in Matthew chapter 18 are followed by church leaders and members, many issues are nipped in the bud before blossoming into larger problems.

Churches are not to function as a spiritual Gestapo. Still, naming Christ's name brings responsibility. Church membership not only offers advantages, but it also brings requirements. God is so serious about His glory that He charges us to love Him and others enough to practice the *hard truth* of church discipline. One of the main reasons for the powerlessness of today's churches is found in disobedience to these instructions laid out in Matthew chapter 18.

REFLECTIONS

1. God has delegated authority to His church. He calls on congregations to share in the process of restoring erring members.

2. The direction in a ministry is not determined by what is taught but by what is tolerated.

3. The goal of church discipline is restoration. The process begins with individuals obeying Christ's instructions.

4. "When church discipline goes out the window, Christ walks out the door."

STUDY QUESTIONS AND POINTS OF APPLICATION

1. Review the four-step strategy given by Christ.

2. God is serious about holiness and purity. Why do you think this passage of Scripture is often neglected?

3. The process begins with individuals. Do you need to privately care-front someone?

SUMMARIZING THE DIFFERENCE BETWEEN FORGIVENESS AND RECONCILIATION

1. It takes one person to forgive.

2. It takes two to be reunited.

3. Forgiving happens inside the wounded person.

4. Reunion happens in a relationship between people.

5. We can forgive a person who never says he is sorry.

6. We cannot be truly reunited unless he is honestly sorry.

7. We can forgive even if we do not trust the person who wronged us once not to wrong us again.

8. Reunion can happen only if we can trust the person who wronged us once not to wrong us again.

9. Forgiving has no strings attached.

10. Reunion has several strings attached.

Written by L. B. Smedes

ENJOYING FORGIVENESS

CHAPTER 18

WHAT ARE THE FRUITS OF FORGIVENESS?

William Arnot, a Bible commentator, tells the story of a traveler in Burma who crossed a river and found his entire body covered by a host of leeches. As the leeches busily sucked his blood, his first reaction was to tear the tormenting creatures from his flesh. But his servant warned him that to do so would place his life in peril. Tearing them off would leave sores that would become seriously infected. The leeches, his servant said, would need to drop off spontaneously to be rendered harmless. The servant prepared a herbal bath for his master. When the master bathed in the balsam, the leeches dropped off. Arnot made application of the story in these words:

Each unforgiven injury rankling in the heart is like a leech sucking the life-blood. Mere human determination to have done with it will not cast the evil thing away. You must bathe your whole being in God's pardoning mercy, and these venomous creatures will instantly let go of their hold. You will stand up free (Mac Arthur, 1984).

What marvelous freedom and relief we find in forgiveness! It brings a joy that wells up within the depths of the soul, overflowing to all around us. It is a joy that cannot be contained; the results are infectious. To forgive is to tap into God's riches. Corrie ten Boom, whose family hid Jews in their home in Holland during the rule of Hitler, deeply knew the joy and fruit of forgiveness. Arrested by the Nazis and sent to a concentration camp, she was the only member of her family to survive the war. Despite the deaths of her loved ones and the unspeakable treatment they suffered at the hands of the Nazis, Corrie refused to hate. She forgave. As a result, God gave her a worldwide ministry that continues to touch the hearts of millions.

RESOLUTION

Matthew 18:15 states: *"Moreover if thy brother shall trespass against thee, go and tell him his fault between thee and him alone: if he shall hear thee, thou hast gained thy brother.*" How wonderful! A brother or sister has been gained! What a precious blessing when brethren are reconciled! No problems are too big to solve—only people too small to solve them. How many devastated marriages could be saved if those involved were willing to forgive and follow steps toward reconciliation? What fellowship families could enjoy if family members would forgive and be reconciled one to another? How many children could be spared from delinquency if moms and dads had been reconciled? How much more blessing would churches know if members were willing to forgive and be reconciled? Reconciliation is one of the tremendous fruits of forgiveness.

Restored relationships are conditional. In order to gain your brother, he must be willing to participate in the process. First, he must be willing to hear you. That means he listens to your concerns and takes the matter to heart. Second, your offender must respond appropriately. When the air is cleared, forgiveness sought and granted, the relationship is salvaged. What a blessing!

Just as God forgives and reconciles the erring sinner, our purpose is to be reconciled to those whom we have forgiven. Our calling is to build bridges, not walls. Nothing gives a parent greater joy than to see his children love one another. And our Heavenly Father experiences great joy when He sees us loving one another too. We see the great truth of Christ's deity in the oneness of God's people. In His high priestly prayer in John chapter 17, our Lord prayed, *"...that they also may be one in us: that the world may believe that thou hast sent me"* (John 17:21). Our goal is to restore, not to alienate. This restoration may not be easy, but it is a great blessing when it occurs.

REVIVAL

Following hard on the heels of reconciliation is revival. Revival is simply getting right with God and others. Being unforgiving is one of the major barricades to revival in our churches. D. L. Moody said, "The one sin that is doing more to hold back the power of God in revival than any other sin is an unforgiving spirit."

Miss Bertha Smith, a veteran missionary during the great Shantung revival in China, testified that revival began when the missionaries were convicted of unforgiving spirits and began to confess their sins one to another and to forgive one another.

Small, petty problems can quickly lead to bitterness and wreak havoc. Scripture warns that *"the little foxes... spoil the vines"* (Song of Sol. 2:15). Soon the power of God's Holy Spirit is shut out from a congregation. But as people begin to confess and forgive, God once again moves in power. A new atmosphere of freedom descends upon congregations when Christians obey God. Cleared consciences soften hard hearts. Peace replaces tension. Joy floods revived souls. When hearts and congregations are cleansed, the Holy Spirit is no longer grieved. It sure is good to be in town when God is!

God cannot show up and show off until there is vertical and horizontal restoration. Revival is not only getting the roof off toward heaven but also getting the walls down between ourselves and others where possible. Many want to get right only with God but not with their brothers and sisters. Yet we must be transparent. Removing walls restores vital reality. And the evidence of this is the attempt to square things between our souls and our brothers.

Joy and Peace

God's reviving presence brings joy. The psalmist prayed in Psalm 85:6: *"Wilt thou not revive us again: that thy people may rejoice in thee?"* Unspeakable joy thrives when God's power is upon His people. We discover a holy epidemic of joy when God's people begin to forgive one another. One of sin's consequences is both inward and outward turmoil. But when the joy of forgiveness comes, peace follows in its wake.

Jesus said, *"Peace I leave with you, my peace I give unto you"* (John 14:27). Matthew Henry shares an interesting comment on the peace the Lord Jesus gives:

When Christ was about to leave this world, He made His will. His soul He committed to His Father; His body He bequeathed to Joseph to be decently interred; His clothes fell to the soldiers; His mother was left to the care of John. But what should He leave His poor disciples? He had no silver or gold, but He left them that which was infinitely better—His peace!

Edwin Markum made a good living as a poet. He entrusted the management of his retirement finances to a banker friend. When Markum neared retirement, he discovered to his surprise that his banker friend had misused the money and lost all of it. Markum felt wounded and betrayed; he had nothing on which to retire. The offense burned within him until he hated his friend and would not forgive him. Trying to write, he sat at his desk for days, but no words would come. Bitterness had poisoned and paralyzed his creative juices. Finally, one day, while sitting at his desk and aimlessly drawing circles on a piece of paper, this thought entered his mind: *If I don't forgive this man, I will destroy myself.* He bowed his head and prayed, "O God, O God, help me; I do forgive him." Instantly the burden lifted, and he penned these words:

He drew a circle that shut me out;

Heretic, rebel, a thing to flout.

But love and I had the will to win—

We drew a circle that took him in.

Edwin Markum continued to write for twenty more years. They were the most productive years of his life; all because he forgave!

Romans 12:18 admonishes us, *"If it be possible, as much as lieth in you, live peaceably with **all men**"* (emphasis added). Jesus said, *"Blessed are the peacemakers"* (Matt. 5:9). We should do all within us by God's grace to live in peace and harmony with others. Sometimes the other party may be unwilling to make peace. In this situation, claim your freedom and move on. Refuse to be trapped in bondage by the reactions of those over whom you have no control. Do right and leave the matter with God. Forgiveness yields the blessed and holy fruit of joy and peace within and without. Some of God's finest gifts become ours when, in obedience, we forgive as Christ forgave.

REFLECTIONS

1. Unforgiveness is like a leech; it sucks the life out of us.

2. Bitterness does more to hold back God's power than any other sin.

3. Jesus prayed for "oneness" among His followers. This supernatural unity in a chaotic culture testifies to a watching world that Christ is indeed divine.

STUDY QUESTIONS AND POINTS OF APPLICATION

1. Review the fruits of forgiveness: resolution, revival, and the restoration of joy and peace.

2. Based on the fruits of forgiveness, write a testimony of a recent experience of obedience in either granting or seeking forgiveness. Consider allowing your pastor to read the testimony and ask him to permit you to share the testimony with the congregation.

3. Do everything within your power to live harmoniously with "all men." But realize that you have no control over the choices of others. Ponder the teaching of Proverbs 16:7 in light of the fact that others may not respond positively: *"When a man's ways please the Lord, he maketh even his enemies to be at peace with him."*

4. How should you respond if someone from whom you have sought forgiveness reacts harshly or refuses to forgive you?

CHAPTER 19

HAS GOD FORGIVEN YOU?

God's goal in the forgiveness He provides through Christ is that of reconciliation. The word *reconcile* means "to be at peace with." *"For if, when we were enemies* [of God], *we were reconciled to God by the death of his Son"* (Rom. 5:10). Our old sin nature is opposed to God. In fact, the Bible says that the fleshly nature wars against God. (See Romans 8:7.) When God forgives a repentant sinner, God reconciles the one who was His enemy before He grants forgiveness. A division no longer exists. The forgiven sinner is at peace with God, reconciled.

Christ's death on Calvary was God's way of paying our debt of offense against a holy God. Man's sin brought the penalty of death. Our sin debt had to be paid, and Christ took that debt upon Himself. He fully satisfied the debt by bearing the loss personally. The Lord Jesus took our sin and its penalty in His own body on the cross. He did not ignore or overlook our debt. He paid the ultimate price by dying in our place and totally satisfying God's justice. Before sinners could be forgiven, sin had to be judged. The debt had to be satisfied. Through Christ's death, the payment has been made, and God is satisfied. One thing God could never accept for sin is an excuse. Your sin will either be pardoned in Christ or forever judged in eternity. In His great love and mercy, God provided the way of forgiveness in His Son.

Alexander, the czar of Russia, once camped with his soldiers on the field. One night after all was quiet and dark, he was walking across the camp among the tents when he saw a light in an officer's tent. Going to the tent and lifting the flap, he saw a young officer sitting at a table with his head down in his arms beside a burning candle. He recognized the officer as a son of the Russian nobility. Entering the tent, Alexander noticed that the officer had a revolver in his hand, yet he was sound asleep. Alexander read the piece of paper on the table and saw a long list of debts. At the bottom, the soldier had added up the sum of his debts and written, "Who can pay so much?" The czar realized the son could not pay the debt. Rather than disgrace his family and name, he was going to take his own life. Alexander picked up the pen and under the question "Who can pay so much?" wrote, "Alexander." Then he left.

Soon the young officer awoke and picked up the revolver to end his life. As he did so, he glanced at the list one more time, all the while feeling greater despair. But, at the bottom of the list, he read, "Alexander." Recognizing the czar's signature, he leaped up from the table and cried, "I'm saved!"

Who could pay so much for our sins? The Lord Jesus did. He suffered in our place, taking our blame upon Himself even though He was innocent. Christ paid a debt He did not owe because we had a debt that was impossible for us to pay.

When men repent of their sins and trust in Jesus Christ, they experience peace with God. What grace that we, as aliens and enemies, may hear God speak peace to our hearts! How do you receive the forgiveness of God? You must come to God with a heart that is broken over your sinfulness, realizing that it is impossible to pay your own debt. You cry out to God for mercy, acknowledging that what you deserve is eternal judgment. And in the midst of your brokenness, God comes in tender grace and forgives you. Only one picture in the Bible describes God running. It is a picture of the father running to forgive and receive his erring child. (See Luke 15.)

Perhaps, like most people, someone has deeply hurt you. Perhaps it was a family member or spouse, or maybe it was a friend or work associate who somehow offended you. For years, you have been waiting for the other person to change. Maybe God is waiting for *you* to change. We cannot drum up forgiveness. Only as we receive God's acceptance and forgiveness for what is in our hearts will we find forgiveness flowing from within us to others. You may discover that instead of being hurt so much, you may be the one who did the hurting. Perhaps you were rejecting, acting unlovingly, being indifferent, and doing the same things you thought others were doing to you. As you confess your sins to the Lord, you can have a broken heart over your own sinfulness. Isn't it true that it is much easier to be brokenhearted over others' sins than to be brokenhearted over your own?

Only as we receive God's forgiveness through Christ will we find the release we desire and must have. We do not forgive others because they are right; we forgive because we want to be right. God allows hurts and offenses to come into our lives because He wants to do something in us to heal us.

The person you react to may be the one God has chosen to use to heal a part of you that so desperately needs His touch. Picture the Lord Jesus Christ beside you right now and beside Him the person who has hurt you most deeply. Hear Him say to you, "I love you. I died for you and everything you've ever done. Will you take My forgiveness? And I know how much this person has hurt you. Will you forgive him for My sake? Instead of focusing on how this person has hurt you, will you not look into your own heart and see what I see there? Let Me forgive, love, and accept you."

Will you respond to Him? How you respond determines not only the course of your relationships for this lifetime but also your eternal destiny.

REFLECTIONS

1. When God forgives a repentant sinner, He reconciles the one who was His enemy before He grants forgiveness.

2. We do not forgive others because they are right; we forgive others because we want to be right.

3. Salvation means Turning from sin to God, Trusting Jesus as Lord and Savior, and Taking God's gift of forgiveness.

STUDY QUESTIONS AND
POINTS OF APPLICATION

1. What is the basis of God's forgiveness? What happened to make this forgiveness possible?

2. If someone asked you to describe how to receive God's forgiveness, what would you say?

3. If you have never turned from sin, recognizing your offenses against a holy God, and trusted in Christ as your Savior, do so now as God speaks to your heart.

CHAPTER 20

HOW DO I KNOW I HAVE FORGIVEN?

As we have seen, a portion of the familiar model prayer says the following: *"And forgive us our debts, as we forgive our debtors"* (Matt. 6:12). If the Lord were to forgive you today the same way you are forgiving others, how would you be forgiven? Perhaps you would not receive much of His forgiveness based on your forgiveness of others. Allow this truth to penetrate your heart. It is God's grace in forgiving us that enables us to forgive others. Forgiving grace is one of the amazing benefits of saving grace. God never asks anything of us except what He, in His grace, grants to us. The Lord never asks us to do anything without giving us the ability to carry out His instructions.

How can you know whether you have really forgiven someone? The ultimate question is simply this: Is God bigger than your hurt? Or will you allow your hurt to be bigger than your God? Ultimately, you will choose the answer for your own life.

It is easy to love God because He is perfect. It is not so easy to love others because none of us comes even close to perfection. Only supernatural empowerment can make possible the forgiving of our fellow, fallible companions. This fact is the reason why the Lord said we will know He is who He is because of our love for one another. There is nothing natural about love. It is supernatural.

During those times when we are literally consumed with how someone has hurt us, we must choose to believe that God's Word is more true than anything we feel. We must obey God and choose to forgive, allowing God, in His time, to bring our emotions into line. Be aware that months may pass before our emotions align with the truth.

FIVE STAGES OF FORGIVENESS

Just when you think this matter of forgiveness is solidly under your belt, something will come into your life and devastate you. You may do all that you know to do and reckon on all the truth you know, but this method will not seem to work. The pain may become overwhelming, and you may see no way out.

Interestingly, just as there are five stages to death and dying, we may identify five stages to forgiveness. Forgiveness is a death: a death to self.

The first stage of death and dying is denial. We deny the reality of our own death when faced with it. The second stage is anger. We blame something or someone for allowing death to destroy us. The third stage is bargaining. We set up conditions that must be fulfilled before we are ready to die. The fourth is depression. We blame ourselves for letting death destroy us. The final stage is acceptance. We look forward to dying.

Incredibly, we go through the same five stages when we are hurt. The first stage is to deny we are hurt. Next, we blame others for hurting us. We then set up conditions that must be met before we will forgive. We blame ourselves for letting others hurt us. And fifth, we learn to look forward to getting beyond and growing from our hurt.

What is helpful to know is that one may become stuck in one of these stages, particularly in the anger and depression stages. Someone who is physically dying can work through these stages by accepting his feelings and sharing them with someone who will listen in a nonjudgmental way. Similarly, when some-one is "dying from unforgiveness," expressing our feel-ings aloud to the Lord may be helpful. This method is precisely what the psalmist used in so many passages. When, like the psalmist, we express our hurts, we hear the sinfulness of our own hearts, and the truth pierces us. In this way, we will recognize that what comes out of our lips is not the fruit of the Spirit.

To Forgive or Not to Forgive

One deacon fell out with another deacon, and the two carried the grudge for years. Finally, the old deacon was on his deathbed. Some of the church people, coming to talk to him, said, "Look, brother, you are about to die. You don't want to meet God this way. Why don't you forgive your brother?"

The deacon asked, "Are you sure I'm dying?" The church leaders replied in the affirmative; the doctors had given him only a few days.

"Now, get it right," they exhorted.

The deacon responded, "Well, you go tell him I for-give him. But I want you to know that if I get well, it's all off!"

That attitude will never do. Here are some tests to determine the genuineness of our forgiveness:

First, are you able to actively and seriously pray for the person you have forgiven? Of course, the prayer may get stuck in your throat, but you must purpose in your heart that you will pray for him every time he comes to mind. By an act of your will, pray God's best for him. Ask the Lord to save him, bless him and his family, and help him.

Second, break down the word *forgiveness*. Ask yourself, "Am I looking *for* a way of *giving* to you? Or am I withholding in my heart?" If you are withholding in your heart, you do not have the spirit of forgiveness God expects. Can you make an investment of some sort in the one you have forgiven? Praying for that person is one way to invest a treasure, or by giving something that is of value to you. That act will prove the sincerity of your forgiveness. The greatest investment you may make is that of acceptance. This acceptance means you will no longer judge him, criticize him in your heart, or express disapproval to him by looks or words. This response often helps the other person to develop a new attitude toward you so healing can take place.

Mark Twain is attributed to have said, "Forgiveness is the fragrance of the violet on the heel of the one who crushed it." Imagine that someone hurts and crushes you. When he walks away, your response should be as though he stepped on a violet. To forgive is to cancel the debt as though it never happened, to wipe the slate clean. This fragrance is one many in our world desperately need to smell.

The third test of forgiveness comes when you hear something harmful about the person you have professed to forgive. Does your heart secretly rejoice in this news? Scripture tells us that this attitude displeases the Lord. (See Proverbs 24:17.) Delighting in his calamity proves that you have not released the debt and made peace in your heart.

When you pass this person on the sidewalk or in the hallway at your church, what thoughts enter your heart? This is the fourth test of forgiveness. While the human mind is not like a computer with information that can be erased, knowledge of the hurt that occurred should not evoke the same hostility as before. Forgiveness has cleansed the person's record in your heart. In time, you will find both the desire and the freedom to love the former offender and to wish him well.

Fifth, can you honestly ask the Lord, "What qualities are You wanting to build into my life through this hurt?" After gaining your brother, can you be genuine enough to seek the counsel of the person you forgave should the Lord persuade you? That person may be able to identify a blind spot and broaden your perspective. If so, this step is a clear indication of spiritual maturity and unpretentious forgiveness.

Forgiveness is the way of the cross. It is the way of death but also the way of abundant life in Christ. The road to spiritual maturity is often painful because its means are contrary to our human nature. But God never speaks in vague, idealistic generalities. He wants us to take Him seriously. In *Mere Christianity*, C. S. Lewis expresses this truth well:

> When He said, "Be perfect," He meant it. He meant that we must go in for the full treatment. It is hard; but the sort of compromise we are all hankering after is harder—in fact, it is impossible. It may be hard for an egg to turn into a bird: it would be a jolly sight harder for it to learn to fly while remaining in the egg. We are like eggs at present. And you cannot go on indefinitely being just an ordinary, decent egg. We must be hatched or go bad... If we let Him—for we can prevent Him, if we choose—He will make the feeblest and filthiest of us into... a dazzling, radiant, immortal creature, pulsating all through with such energy and joy and wisdom and love as we cannot now imagine, a bright stainless mirror which reflects back to God perfectly (though of course, on a smaller scale) His own boundless power and delight

and goodness. The process will be long and in parts very painful; but that is what we are in for. Nothing less.

God means what He said. Forgiveness is God's mandate, the way of the cross, the key to human relationships, the joy of growth, victorious living, and the way to enjoy life on earth. Applying these principles is your key to mastering the art of forgiveness. The power of forgiveness is amazing. No, not everyone will choose to get along with you, but you can do your part to get along with them!

REFLECTIONS

1. Forgiving grace is one of the amazing benefits of saving grace. God never asks anything of us except what He, in His grace, grants to us.

2. "Forgiveness is the fragrance of the violet on the heel of the one who crushed it."

STUDY QUESTIONS AND POINTS OF APPLICATION

1. Consider the impact of the following statement from this chapter: "During those times when we are literally consumed with how someone hurt us, we must choose

to believe that God's Word is more true than anything we feel." How would this statement apply to your response toward someone who has hurt you deeply?

2. Someone has observed that "God has never used anyone greatly until He has first hurt him deeply." What is God's ultimate purpose in allowing others to hurt, offend, or wrong us? How does our response to hurts affect the working out of God's purpose in our lives?

3. This chapter lists five stages of forgiveness. Considering the deepest hurt you have ever experienced, at which stage are you? As needed, seek the Lord to enable you to proceed to the next stage of growth.

4. Honestly determine the answers to the following tests of your forgiveness:

    - What is your first thought when you hear something harmful about the person you forgave?

    - What is your first thought when you meet someone you have forgiven?

    - Are you able to pray for the one you forgave? Do so now.

CLOSING SUMMARY

Forgiveness is *not* pretending that you are not hurt and angry. Neither is it an attempt to ignore your emotions. Time alone will not heal your wounds. The path to restoration is not automatic, nor is it magical or mystical. Action is required to break free from the prison of offense. Mastering the art of forgiveness requires three steps:

#1 Discern the Root. Stop living in denial. You should not feel guilty about the wrongs others have inflicted upon you. Before you can heal, you need to have the courage to confront your pain. Also, you may need to confront those who did you wrong. This is difficult but necessary.

#2 Dissect the Fruit. Your anger and depression may be due to wounds from the past. Identify the root of your unhealed hurts. Name your abusers. Make a one-time list. If needed, bring your case to the proper legal authorities. Spiritual men and women are available to assist you. Take advantage of those who have wisdom and experience in these matters.

#3 Delete the Suit. Finally, close the legal file on that episode from your past. Settle it in your heart and walk away. Release the debts you are holding against your offenders. Then destroy your list of hurts and offenses. Turn your case over to the Lord. Allow Him to mete out His justice in His time. When you choose to forgive, you are freed from the prison of offense. You are on the road to healing. Someone said, "The school-of-suffering graduates are rare scholars." Your healing qualifies you to assist others who are facing similar circumstances. God can heal your broken heart and set you free. Refuse to allow this to drag on. Discern it. Dissect it. Delete it!

REFERENCES

Carnegie, D. (2010). *How to Stop Worrying and Start Living*. NY: Simon & Schuster.

Cousins, N. (1979). *Anatomy of an Illness*. New York: Open Road Media.

Davis, R. L. (n.d.). *Mistreated*. Portland, Oregon: Multnomah, 1989, pp. 19-20.

Henry, M. (1721). *Matthew Henry's Commentary*. Old Tappan, NJ: Fleming H. Revell Company.

Lewis, C. S. (1952). *Mere Christianity*. Westwood, NJ, USA: Macmillian Incorporated.

Mac Arthur, J. J. (1984). *The Elements of Church Discipline*. Panorama City, CA: Word of Grace Communications.

Mandella, N. (2013, 12 6). Interview. *Los Angeles Times.*

Medicine, S. b. (2022, February 7). Johns Hopkins Medicine. Retrieved from Forgiveness: Your Health Depends on It: https://www.hopkinsmedicine.org/health/wellness-and-prevention/forgiveness-your-health-depends-on-it

Moody, D. L. (April 21, 2020). *Prevailing Prayer: What Hinders It?* eBook release. Chicago: F.H. Revell.

Pope, A. (1733-1734). *Essay on Man, Epistle II.* Public Domain.

Smedes, L. B. (1997). *The Art of Forgiving: When You Need to Forgive and Don't Know How.* Random House Publishing.

Spurgeon, C. (2004). *Waging War in the Light of God's Revelation.* (R. R. Hundley, Ed.) USA: Xulon Press, Copyright © 2004. Retrieved 2022

ABOUT HAROLD VAUGHAN

Harold Vaughan is the founder of Christ Life Ministries. The ministry has three main emphases: Prayer Advance Conferences, Publications, and Preaching. His itinerant ministry has allowed him to preach in forty-eight states and many foreign countries. Local church events include REVIVAL SUMMITS, PRAYER SUMMITS, HOME IMPROVEMENT CONFERENCES, and the IRON MAN CONFERENCE. He carries a burden for revival and prayer.

Christ Life Ministries, founded by Harold Vaughan, is committed to promoting personal and corporate revival in the local church. Our resources include materials, messages, and ministries to aid you in your Christian walk. To learn more about the plethora of available help go to...

www.ChristLifeMin.org